MOP MEN

MOP MEN

Inside the World of
Crime Scene Cleaners

Alan Emmins

THOMAS DUNNE BOOKS ﾷﾷ NEW YORK
ST. MARTIN'S PRESS

THOMAS DUNNE BOOKS.
An imprint of St. Martin's Press.

MOP MEN. Copyright © 2004, 2008 by Alan Emmins. All rights reserved.
Printed in the United States of America. For information, address St. Martin's
Press, 175 Fifth Avenue, New York, N.Y. 10010.

www.thomasdunnebooks.com
www.stmartins.com

Design by Phil Mazzone

Library of Congress Cataloging-in-Publication Data

Emmis, Alan, 1974–
    Mop men : inside the world of Crime Scene Cleaners / Alan Emmins.—
1st U. S. ed.
        p.   cm.
    ISBN-13: 978-0-312-53274-1
    ISBN-10: 0-312-53274-1
    1. Crimes—United States. 2. Crime scenes—United States. 3. Crime
Scene Cleaners (Firm) I. Title.
    HV6529.E46 2009
    364.1520973—dc22
                                                    2008029879

First published in Great Britain by Corvo Books.

First U.S. Edition: January 2009

10 9 8 7 6 5 4 3 2 1

For Matt Dougherty

CONTENTS

PRAYING FOR DEATH   1

A DUDE GOT HIS FREAK ON   7

FEAR AND LOATHING IN SANTA CRUZ   19

DUDE I'M DYING . . . CHA-CHING!   35

THUMB MAN CHRONICLES   61

M IS FOR MOGUL   69

MAN IN THE BATH PART I—THE VIRGIN AND THE FLY   89

HEPATITIS C YOU LATER   101

THE CAVALIER MAN   137

THE DARK LORD PERFORMS A JEDI MIND TRICK   143

Contents

MAN IN THE BATH PART II—I KNEW YOU WERE COMING   153

DEATH AND DAYS OFF   171

COOLER THAN ELVIS   179

SELLING TO THE FUTURE DEAD   181

SELLING TO THE RELATIVES OF THE DEAD   189

GOING ONCE . . . GOING TWICE . . . GONE   199

CRANK HOUSE   211

MAN IN THE BATH PART III—THE STATE VS JAMES MCKINNON   219

WHEN IT RAINS IT POURS   233

MAN IN THE BATH PART IV   241

MISS MISERY   263

MISCREANTS ON THE LOOSE   275

SITTING NAKED IN THE FOREST   291

EPILOGUE: MAN IN THE BATH PART V   297

MOP MEN

AUTHOR'S NOTE

This is a true story, though some names and details have been changed.

PRAYING FOR DEATH

I had a meeting with the editor of a lifestyle magazine. I was pitching a story covering one of the lantern festivals in Taiwan—a cultural gala held for the gods that ends in pyrotechnic lunacy. When the locals settle down for the evening, crash-helmeted youths take to the streets in an attempt to remove one another's heads with fifty-dollar rockets. The editor raised an eyebrow. It was clear that, for the first time since sitting down, I had his full attention. He looked so excited, as he sat there scribbling notes, that I assumed the story was in the bag. Flight tickets needed to be booked, lightweight shirts and a pair of good-quality safety goggles needed purchasing.

"Do people die?" he asked.

"Not that I'm aware of," I replied, slightly amused by the directness of the question.

The editor slumped back in his seat without even a cursory attempt at hiding his disappointment. We moved on quickly to the next pitch, but I never got his full attention again. *If only one of the pesky little brats would die,* I thought, *I could be on my way to Taiwan.*

But it was not to be. Of the five stories I was pitching that day none of them offered a single death, and, so it seemed, none of the stories were commissioned. It was an error on my part. This was a men's lifestyle magazine. I knew they wanted entertainment, I just hadn't realized at that point just how entertaining death was.

I was so out of tune with death that I didn't even see the stories when I was virtually tripping over them. Shortly after the editorial pitch, when leaving my apartment building, I came across a man wearing a balaclava and clasping a gun. He was lying facedown in the street. I did not run back upstairs for my camera or indeed even smell a story. I just walked by, mumbling the words *fucking idiot.*

For me, a dead body outside my front door was simply not possible. This wasn't my life. This kind of thing didn't happen in my neighborhood. This was Copenhagen, land of rickety bicycles and beautiful women. Gunmen? Get out of here! So I stepped over the bugger, looking around for the camera, totally believing this was some kind of stupid *Candid Camera* thing. I wasn't going to be the idiot being laughed at on some cheesy cable show. Oh, no. Not me. *Watch, I am just going to step over him and go about my business.*

When I returned five minutes later, the whole street was taped off. It was real. The man had been in a shootout outside a hash club one street away from my apartment. He had been shot in the stomach, had stumbled away and then collapsed outside my building.

The only photograph in the papers the next day was of his red balaclava, alone and stranded in the road.

Even then I didn't get it. It wasn't until I relayed the story to one of my friends, who said, "And you call yourself a journalist?" that I thought, *Yeah, maybe I should stop calling myself* that.

A few weeks later the penny finally dropped. I woke up with the eye-popping realization that death was a money machine. I found myself writing an article on gaming, and while reading through a gaming magazine I came across the following ad copy for the WingMan Force joystick:

Psychiatrists say it's important to feel something when you kill. When you kill without feeling, you're just another heartless sociopath. That's why you need Logitech's WingMan Force Joystick . . .

That's right. *You* can feel the recoil of the gun. *You* can straddle the boundary between reality and fiction. I was blown away by the advert, even admired the cleverness of how it spoke to its target audience. Yet, at the same time, and also for the very same reason, I was appalled by it. Part of me couldn't believe it had actually been allowed into print, into a publication read by impressionable youths. On another level, even though I am not and can't imagine that I ever will be a gamer, it spoke directly to me. It made me realize that if I was going to continue making my living writing feature articles for lifestyle magazines, I would have to master this death-as-entertainment business. I was going to have to get closer to Death, maybe even carry his scythe.

My subsequent investigations didn't lead me to Death himself. Instead, they led me to a man named Neal Smither, who, if not actually one of Death's litter, must be at the bare minimum a cousin.

On any given day Neal Smither can be found swinging about on the velvety coattails of Death's outer garment; grinning like a man who has just hatched a master plan for world domination, screaming the words *Praying for death, baby!* to the many and varied media outlets that form orderly queues in front of him. This death he prays for is not his own, but *yours*. You see, Death and Neal Smither, as well as being related, are in the same line of business. It's as if Death, after one day splattering somebody against the wall of a recently decorated living room, stood back, admired the bloody mess, and thought, *There's coin to be made here.*

Neal's company is called Crime Scene Cleaners, Inc. His slogan, the tagline that sits beneath the name on the side of his truck, is: HOMICIDES, SUICIDES & ACCIDENTAL DEATHS. Neal makes his living cleaning up the remains of the less fortunate. Whichever route into the bright light you may take, however messy the tunnel may become, Neal will happily clean you up for a standard fee.

"What can I tell ya, buddy? It's better I do it than mom and pop, 'cause they don't wanna be on their hands and knees collecting bits of skull fragment. They don't wanna scrub the brains off the wall that little Johnny Dirtbag left behind just after he hit the crack pipe and stuck a twelve-gauge in his mouth."

Even if harshly put, it is a fair point. Even the most skilled of debating teams would struggle to form a convincing, contrary argument.

Neal is about five feet six and drives a gigantic black truck with blacked-out windows. His short, dark hair is nearly always hidden under a baseball cap. Salesmanship is everything. Neal even speaks with a Texas accent because he says the southern drawl sounds more "honest," more disarming. Neal, however, is from Capitola, California. He and Crime Scene Cleaners, Inc., are based in the San Francisco Bay Area.

My first reaction to Neal when I met him was one of shock. Where was the politeness associated with death? Where was the calm, polite guy who cleaned up the bloody mess to spare the loved ones the hurt and the pain? When I first called Neal to ask if I could write an article about him, I asked him what he was doing there and then.

"Oh, you know, same old, same old. Just sitting here praying for death, hoping some scumbag's got the razor blade in his hand right about now."

From my very first phone conversation with Neal, I knew his story was going to be an easy sell. I didn't even try to place the article beforehand. I had no doubt that I would have a choice of buyers for this story. I focused on more immediate issues. Flight tickets needed to be booked, lightweight shirts and possibly a pair of good-quality safety goggles needed purchasing. A couple of days later I flew from New York to San Francisco and with an unplanned tire screech set off for the black dot I had penned on my map.

A DUDE GOT HIS FREAK ON

Two hours later, I was three steps behind Neal as he entered a motel room where somebody had recently committed suicide.

At that precise moment, as the motel door was pushed open, I was the happiest little feature writer on the planet.

I was in San Francisco.

I was loving my job.

"What we got? Oh, looky here! Chicks with dicks," said Neal as we sauntered into the middle of the motel room. "Dude even brought his own DVD player. That shit's a newer model than mine. Can you believe that shit?"

Neal surveyed the room while holding on to several DVD cases with covers for transvestite porn. On the bed the contents of a bag had been poured out. There were several porn magazines, the newest issue of *Transformation*, lots of unopened bills, and a lone and somewhat beached-looking rubber breast. On the table by the wall was an upturned, powder-encrusted vial that looked as if it had held cocaine. The table itself had a film of white dust over most of its surface. There were two coffee cups, an empty carton of Parliament cigarettes, and a packet of pills that had been half emptied. In one of the cups, floating in water, were some of the pills.

While the bed looked like something left by an unruly teenager who couldn't wait to go out and see his friends, the table showed sadness. A dusty white void of loneliness befitting a room where somebody had recently killed himself. There's no telling why the occupant had decided to take his own life. Was it the unpaid bills? Or was it some deeper sexual turmoil? You and I will never know. You and I don't need to know. Analyzing why will not alter the underlying fact that the man was dead and Neal was there to clean up the mess left behind. All we knew was that the occupant's name was James.

"Fuck. Dude got his freak on! One last freaky blowout before he went. *Fucking freak!* You see the table there, Alan? You know what that is?" asked Neal. "*Crack!*"

I was somewhat confused as I stood there checking out my surroundings, trying to get a sense of the energy left behind in the room. While I'd been scoping out the scene, Neal had done nothing but scope out the porn, laughing callously as he called out the titles and tossed the cases one by one onto the bed. But once the porn inspection had been completed Neal became confused. He paced around the room, searching. This was odd. The initial phone call had said that there was lots of blood to clean up. Yet, the room, while disheveled, was not at all bloody.

"Maybe the fucker OD'd—I hate the bitches that OD. I

can't make any money off an OD!" said Neal as he pushed the bathroom door slowly open. "Oh, I take it back, you *weren't* a bitch. Come take a look at this, Alan—this is ya typical bleeder."

I froze for a second. My only contact with death to date had been the death of my grandmother when I was sixteen. There was nothing visually disturbing about her death. Not for me, at least. It was clean. A wooden box and a set of sliding doors that closed behind her were all I had to deal with. Whatever was awaiting me in that motel bathroom was going to represent death in a way that I knew nothing about. Suddenly I had a reality check. I wasn't sure if it was a line I was ready to cross. My only certainty was that I would find it easier to deal with if Neal was not talking his talk as I tiptoed into the room.

Just twenty-four hours ago the bathroom would have been white. This was a national motel chain, meaning that while basic and plain in design, it would have been generally clean. The room would have been cleaned every day. This place couldn't have been more than a few years old. Looking at the fittings between all the splattered blood, I got the impression that the room scrubbed up pretty well. And it would take some scrubbing. Everything was tainted: the walls, the shower booth and fittings, the sink, the toilet, and the floor were all smeared with blood. In some places the blood went all the way to the top of the walls, not quite reaching the ceiling, but almost. Most of it was just splashed around, except for the floor, which was covered with bloody footprints—patterns made with bare feet, as in a child's painting. There was a telephone mounted on the wall next to the toilet. Why do they do that? I wondered. I didn't want anybody calling me when they were on the toilet. But maybe it was for situations such as this one. Is it possible that the telephone was mounted there with the suicidal in mind? Maybe hotel management had learned from experience that if you put a phone in the bathroom the suicides won't walk out into the bedroom with their slit wrists bleeding all over the carpet. That they will remain contained on the easy-to-clean tiled floor?

"That's pretty, ain't it? You see the phone?" Neal asked as he hovered in the doorway. "That's pretty typical—fuckers slit their wrists and as soon as they've done it they wanna call somebody up to tell them all about it."

I was starting to freak out a little. I was a long way from my comfort zone. I stood staring at the blood, wishing I could pretend it was something else. In fact, if Neal Smither would have just shut up for a minute, I was pretty convinced that I could separate myself from the reality. But Neal wouldn't shut up.

"You gonna take any pictures or are you just gonna stand there?" asked the indelible Neal Smither.

Neal is so harsh a character that once he has entered your head you will remember him for the rest of your life. He is like a bad stain that you can't scrub away. When the time comes to face your own death, Neal, if you have met him, will no doubt be on your mind. I am certain he will be there at the forefront of my own mental commentary when I die. In fact, I am already convinced that Death himself will be wearing a Crime Scene Cleaners, Inc., T-shirt.

I moved around the bathroom, trying to skirt the blood as I took pictures. It was hard for me to work out what I felt about this loss of life. My ego was in the way. The answer was too dependent on what kind of person I was, or, more to the point, what kind of person I wanted to be. Did I feel for this wasted life? Was it a tragedy? Or was I simply indifferent to it? I looked through the lens of my camera and pondered as I snapped away, aware that I should care, slightly aware that I didn't, but very aware that I wanted to switch to my wide-angle lens so that I could get more of the blood in the frame. Only now, looking back, can I honestly say I had no feelings at all. I knew nothing of this life. To me it wasn't even a life, it was just blood on a wall, fingerprints on the phone—a guy called James whom I had never met. It was an article I was going to make money on. But Neal's crassness made me feel like I should have cared. If I didn't, who would? Did someone like James have any loved ones? If he felt the need to lock himself in a strange room and cut his own wrists, he clearly didn't think so. But without putting a face to the death, a body maybe, what can you feel? It's just blood on a wall.

"Alan, if you want any of that porn you should just take it, it's just gonna get thrown out otherwise," offered Neal.

I was wondering when I would find time to pickup gifts for friends, but I didn't think transgender porn stolen from a dead guy was a suitable gift for anybody.

The motel room door clicked and opened. A tall, thin, well-groomed man in his midthirties poked his head around the door. He was wearing a yellow tie with red dots, which he stroked nervously while he spoke.

"Do you have any idea how long you guys are going to be? This room is booked out."

Booked out? I thought to myself. There was a guy's

blood on the floor, drugs were smeared across the table, and a rubber breast lay on the bed. Could he let this room out? Was it legal? Was there not supposed to be some kind of cool-off period? An exorcism at the very least? No, apparently not. If it's clean it's available. *It was a gallant effort, James, but corporate America is not about to let you screw with a schedule,* I thought.

"Two hours max," said Neal, taking on a more serious tone. "He was good enough to stay in the bathroom, so this will be fast and easy."

"Just the way you like it," I said flippantly to the manager. A laugh slipped out as I spoke. I really was referring to the availability of the room. But for some inappropriate reason I was struck by the sexual innuendo. It was the kind of put-down two friends in a bar might banter with. I knew it was wrong—both to say what I had said and to then laugh about it, but there was no keeping it in. The fact that neither Neal nor the manager batted an eyelid sent me into a fit of schoolboy guffaws that I had to smother with my hand as I turned and walked back into the main room.

"Okay," the manager said after a few seconds. "Well, just as soon as you can."

I was relieved as I sensed that the manager was about to leave. But then I heard Neal speak again.

"Did you see the porn?" he asked the manager.

"Yes, I saw the porn," the manager said with an air of impatience as he stood wondering where this conversation was going. Even I was intrigued enough to edge back toward the bathroom so as not to miss anything. After a short but pregnant pause, Neal looked the manager straight in the eye.

"Do you want to take any of it?" he asked.

"Just put everything in the garbage!" The manager, unamused, turned and slammed the door behind him.

"Jeeeeeez, Alan!" Neal said as I tried to control my laughter. "You can't insult my clients like that."

"Neal, I really never meant to." I told him. "I really didn't mean it like that. It just came out wrong."

"I know, I know. I'm not sweating it, dude. Did you see his face? He didn't think that was funny, dude. But then he didn't think the porn was funny either. Christ! Lighten up, Mr. Manager Dude!"

Neal was on his knees in the bathroom. He was wearing a blue all-in-one protective suit and yellow rubber gloves. In his right hand he had a bottle of chemical enzyme that he kept pumping up with pressure before spraying it over the floor. He squirted small areas and then with tissue began to mop up the blood. Like a window cleaner, Neal sang to while away the time as he worked.

Whether it's a scabby knee or a hanging head
We don't care just as long as you're dead
We'll clean on our knees happily
Just as long as your check clears the bank

Good God! I thought as a shockwave pulsed through my body. *What a nasty bastard.* The magazine editors will love you.

Neal worked fast, scrubbing at some of the tougher patches of blood with his brush, humming his joyful ditties as he went. He was sweating a lot, but didn't take a second to wipe his brow.

"You see, Alan," he began without looking up, "I couldn't

give a fuck about scumbags like this. If you take your own life you're a weak, selfish scumbag. You know what I'm saying? You're not thinking about ma and pa who have to then go around and deal with all your freaky shit that you left behind. You saw the porn out there. This guy was a freak. Fuck him. If he wanted to die, good. I'm glad he made a mess."

"But don't you feel any sympathy, Neal?" I asked, shocked that he was talking like this to a journalist with a minidisk recorder in his hand.

"I feel sorry for the parents, you know, who have to deal with this. The maid, too—she didn't wake up this morning and ask for this freak to be dead in one of her rooms. She didn't ask for this freaky fuck to bleed to death on the toilet. But do I really care?" There was a pause here. You could almost hear strings snapping as Neal tried to work out if he cared. "No! I mean how could I? I don't know this person from Adam, you know, and from what I have seen I wouldn't want to, either. But this is how I make my living. If I cared about death, if I started to think about that shit, I couldn't do my job, and I like my job. I work hard. I earn a shitload of money for it and I don't want anybody else doing it. It's as simple as that, dude!"

We didn't talk much after that. Neal concentrated on what he was doing. He scrubbed and wiped for the next hour and for the most part I watched. All the tissue was eventually put in a waste bag. Neal went back into the bathroom for one last inspection, where he got down on his hands and knees and peered into every nook and cranny.

"You really have to check your work in this job," Neal said as he carried out his search. "You'd be amazed how blood just gets itself into places you would never expect.

The last thing you want to do in this game is to leave blood behind."

Satisfied, Neal burst out of the room carrying his own equipment and the waste bag full off bloody tissue. He breezed into the lobby, had them sign a piece of paper, and wished the staff a nice day as he dashed for the door.

A month later, I was back in my apartment in Copenhagen, reading e-mails. There was one from *Rolling Stone* magazine, telling me that they wanted the Crime Scene Cleaner story and that they would make me an offer within the next few days. There was another e-mail from *Penthouse*. They wanted to know if this story had been published before and, if not, where should they send the contract. They wanted worldwide rights and their offer was by far the largest amount I had ever been offered for an article. But, in the end, I didn't sell the story to *Penthouse* or *Rolling Stone*. An editor friend in Denmark suggested that instead of selling worldwide rights, I sell the story country by country. This is what I did, and as more and more sales were confirmed I gave myself a mental pat on the back. With sales in more than fifteen countries, it was confirmed that I really had learned how to deliver death-as-entertainment. So that was that. For my part, it had been a job well done and I would not have to give Neal Smither another thought ever again.

When the payments for the story started to arrive I remember thinking that it had been worth it. Neal may have been an unbearable bugger, but I'd had the last laugh. I'd work with assholes more often, I thought, if I could earn that much every time.

I did manage to forget about Neal for a while, but he continued to niggle at me from time to time. I'd pass a four-car pile up on the highway and I'd imagine Neal peering through the shattered window of a wrecked car: "Ooooh! *Nice!*" he'd say. There'd be a movie on TV with a gruesome murder scene and I'd think: *Neal could have that cleaned up in no time.* I'd see an episode of *CSI* and I'd chuckle, "They need to cast Neal in this program. He could act. He *is* an act."

Seeing Neal as an act struck me like a thunderbolt. Neal had shown me several articles that the American press had written about him and his methods. At the time, I thought he was being used and was too dumb to see it. But maybe the media wasn't using Neal as I had previously thought. Maybe Neal was using the media. Maybe he had used the media's appetite for death to promote his company. All that "praying for death" business—he knew exactly what the media would do with that. He knew exactly what *I* would do with that. I started to wonder if I had done Neal an injustice.

An image of Neal with the transgender porn popped back into my head. It wasn't the image of him laughing or offering the porn to the motel manager. It was an image of him putting the porn in with some other rubbish.

"His family will be pretty upset as it is. They don't need to deal with this stuff."

Had I got him completely wrong? In among all the blood and gore, had I completely missed the real story? Maybe there was something more relevant. A story about how modern society deals with death? Or about how we seem to use death, be entertained by death, and have even managed to turn it into a commodity?

These questions began to circulate in my head with more frequency. But no matter how often I asked them, I never could find reasonable answers. I did begin to realize, though, that as a writer I'd messed up. I'd cashed in and had remained totally blind to any idea that there might have been another, much more interesting story connected to Neal Smither.

Once again I was on the phone booking a plane ticket. I had decided to go back and do this story properly.

Which leads me to the here and now: L.A. airport, where I am trying to fend off a nineteen-year-old Buddhist who is offering to autograph his hardback book, not for a fee, but a donation of fifteen dollars. He follows me with his incessant chatter while I look for a sign for where I should catch the shuttle bus that will take me to my rental car. But I don't mind. I have an enormous grin on my face. I am very happy to be back. I am even looking forward to seeing Neal.

FEAR AND LOATHING IN SANTA CRUZ

As I sit in my hired, white Chevy Cavalier, poorly refreshed from a bad night's sleep in a dirty motel, I realize that I can't remember whether it's Route 1 or Route 101 that follows the ocean from L.A. all the way to San Francisco. I stop in three different gas stations as I head out of town, but they have only local maps, and not the state map I am looking for. Eventually I ask a pair of mechanic's legs that poke out from beneath a yellow truck, and a muffled voice assures me it's Route 101 that I'm looking for. I hear snippets about a bunch of rights and lefts that I need to take, and once again I slip the car into Drive.

The drive from L.A. to San Francisco is breathtaking from the very beginning. Even before you get out of Malibu you have the ocean on your left, dotted with million-dollar beach houses, and imposing orange cliffs that tower over you on the right. Pretty soon you are climbing up into the mountains where you are confronted by an unmeddled-with landscape. Even after the long flight and no sleep, as I look at these grand views, I realize I can't remember when I last felt so awake, so alive.

It's exactly what I need before I slip into four death-coated weeks.

Still, the vast open landscape can be a little intimidating to city eyes that are used to signs for Starbucks and McDonald's blocking their vision. As my eyes flick and dart around in a bid to take in all the unfamiliar contours, I become aware of the adrenaline rush. I am experiencing the kind of excitement that comes when there is a hint of danger. I am, after all, driving an unfamiliar car on what is for me the wrong side of an unfamiliar road. To my left there's a precipice that could send me free-falling into a beautiful abyss, but, sadly, one that ends eventually with a rather tragic and life-ending crunch.

I watch the locals as they whiz by in the other direction, or drive up close behind me, frustrated by my slow and cautious pace. They no longer see what I see. The beautiful landscapes have become run-of-the-mill to those who live with them.

I call Neal to remind him that I am driving up and will be with him the following day. I get his answering service; they tell me that he, too, is driving back from L.A. Instantly I am on the lookout for his big black truck. I imagine him passing me on the inside at a hundred miles per hour. I see myself chasing after him, just for sport, honking my horn and waving as I pull up alongside him. The image I have of Neal is this: He would look at me down there in my little white rental car and mutter something along the lines of "What does this motherfucker want?" before dragging his steering wheel sharply to the right and banging my car off the 101, down a gorge, and into an eventual fireball that would burn me to a crisp and render Neal's services, frustratingly for him, unnecessary.

I exit the 101 for gas and another attempt at buying a map, aware that while the views are still very impressive, I left the ocean some sixty miles back and am still suspicious about Route 101 being the right choice. With my purchase in hand, I stroll over to a tanker driver who is delivering fuel and ask him for some navigational assistance. He is a big bald-headed man with a drooping mustache and tattoos up his arms. He has the look of a guy who, in a movie, would be playing the part of a convicted killer.

"Oh, cool, you want to go through the Big Sur and up that way, huh? You should keep your camera handy. Well, look, we're here. . . ."

I'm not far off course. Route 1 and Route 101 cross each other regularly on the journey to San Francisco. All I need to do, in fact, is continue for another ten miles or so and I will run into signs for Route 1, the correct route. I swing the car around and head for the exit of the gas station. But, as I do, the truck driver walks in front of me and gestures for me to stop.

"Can you do me a favor?" he asks.

Favor? What can it be, this favor? I only asked him for some simple directions and now I find myself indebted to the bugger.

"Of course," I smile.

"Drive real safe when you're out there," he says in earnest.

"It's a real winding, treacherous road with some real steep drops. Just . . . you know, enjoy the view, but be careful."

Well, I'll be damned, I think to myself as I drive off. *Oh, what a cynical asshole am I.* Why, in my mind, did he have to want something? All he wanted was for me to be safe, to not kill myself through stupid driving.

I decided to make this drive because I wanted to go through some kind of mental purification. I know what lies ahead in San Francisco: blood, ghastliness, death, pity, and a rather loud Neal Smither. I need this drive as preparation, to cleanse me, to bring me to the project as open and refreshed as I can possibly be. I feel that if I haven't emptied my head of the things that clutter a daily life, there will not be room for what I am soon to deal with. As I cruise around the valleys, I know that this drive along the ocean was the right move.

California must have some of the most stunning landscapes in the world, and the views from Route 1, with the ocean constantly moving and coming at you from all angles, must be the most stunning of the state. One minute I am at eye level with the water; the next, the ocean languishes at the bottom of a thousand-foot cliff. For so long I have been driving through the mist, unable to see more than twenty feet in front of me on the winding cliff edges, but now the sun is breaking through again. Instead of mist, as I coast around a 180-degree edge, I am greeted once again with the bright blue sky of California.

When the next opportunity presents itself, I pull over into a lookout point. I notice a guy sitting on a boulder; he has a big unkempt dog with him and a cardboard sign. The sign looks out of place up on the cliffs. For the last thirty minutes I have not seen another car going in my direction. Maybe five max going the other way. That figure reduced to the amount of people who stop at *this* viewpoint and then reduced again to actual people willing to give money to a homeless guy reduces all the way down to pretty much nobody.

"How long have you been up here?" I ask him, digging into my pockets.

" 'Bout four months. Van broke down. Just trying to get back home to Pismo Beach."

He is in camouflage from head to foot, clearly hungry, and glad of his dog's company. His big black beard is matted. His sunken eyes are framed by gritty creases. Sweat streaks have made tracks on his skin. His eyes have an acrid glint, reflecting all the new and expensive sports cars that have stopped at this viewpoint over the last four months. They reflect the couples who jumped out of their cars giggling while holding a camera at arm's length to snap a self-portrait, as one such couple is doing now. The couple jumps back in the convertible and wheel-spins away, looking at me as they go as if to say, "Schmuck!"

"Probably *die* up here," the guy with the sign says as the dust from the wheel spin drifts around us. He reaches out and takes the five-dollar bill from my hand. I can't imagine where he might spend these five dollars up here on a mountainside. So, unless his van is alive and well, waiting for him at the next viewpoint—meaning he has just scammed me of five bucks—there's a good chance he will die up here. There's an awkward pause as these thoughts pass through my head and I find myself hoping that he *has* just scammed me. I don't know if I have ever met a valid candidate for suicide before, but as I stand next to this man, both of us looking out over the vast ocean, I feel I have now. But what makes him, in my eyes, a candidate for suicide? Is it just his sadness that pushes me to connect him with death? Do people commit suicide because of something as simple, real, and necessary as sadness?

I have always felt that suicide was connected to communication. Not due to a lack of opportunity, but to an impossibility to communicate and be understood. It can be frustrating to try to share something with somebody, something important and real to you, and see in the face of another person that he either doesn't care or, worse still, simply doesn't understand you. Of course, it is inevitable that this will happen from time to time, but imagine if it were always that way. Imagine if every time you tried to communicate and connect with another human being you fell short. If you never make any sense to anybody, if you never connect, you hold no value: you are truly alone. There are those who can survive as genuine outsiders, and then there are those who can't.

The man here on the boulder is alone in regard to human company. He has these landscapes, sure, but going by the expression on his face, the absurdity of it, it's not enough. He is an outsider himself, but he seems not to be a surviving outsider. I find myself wondering how long he has left.

There's no escaping death in life. I had, however, truly expected to at least forget death on my little road trip from L.A. to S.F., but it seems that even here, on a journey that for the most part is unpopulated, there is no getting away from it. I find myself angry for stopping here. I am angry at having met this man, because now I feel like I can't leave him. I should drive him to Pismo Beach.

Would that save him or just delay something inevitable?

Who knows? Maybe he doesn't need saving; maybe this is me getting ahead of myself, putting myself into somebody else's mind. But still, when I look at him I can't escape the vision of him scooping up his dog and sprinting off the edge of the cliff.

The silence we share as he sits looking at the sea, and I sit wondering about his chances of survival, is strangely calm. It doesn't feel awkward. It's just two strangers sharing a beautiful view, one wondering if the other will die soon.

I say good-bye to the man, pat the dog on the head, and go about my own business.

Should I have done more? I wonder as I wind my way along the road. Probably. So much for cleansing myself of death. Instead, here I am worrying that I have just left this lonely and stranded guy to commit suicide. I pull into the next viewpoint and study the map. Pismo Beach is even on my way. I could.

But I have seen this camouflage-clad, bearded outsider before: he's been in dozens of movies, as have I, the guilt-tripped unsuspecting idiot with a car and an empty passenger seat.

I drive back to the last viewpoint, willing myself to turn around and not do this. But something keeps me going. I don't want this guy to commit suicide.

Of course, I wouldn't know either way. But I would know that I had not offered to help him travel in a direction in which I am going anyway.

And now, as I look at the boulder where he once sat, I can see that I never will know, because the boulder is now empty. I am half tempted to get out of the car to see if I can find a set of footprints running off the edge of the cliff. But I don't. I smile and think, *Enjoy the five dollars you just scammed from me,* and drive off once again in the direction of San Francisco, promising myself I will think no more of death until I am face-to-face with Neal Smither.

After nine hours of driving I make it to Santa Cruz, where, tired and terribly lonely from my time in the car, I am going to spend the night. I had had plans of finding somewhere nice to stay, but having got myself stuck on a traffic-jammed one-way system, with no idea where it goes, I give up on the idea. I am tired and hungry and pull into the first cheap motel I see.

I dump my bags in the room and quickly head out for food. I walk toward the ocean, imagining a cold beer in a pretty little beachside café. Any of you who know Santa Cruz will know that this is a notion of utter madness. The part of Santa Cruz where I find myself looks like a meth slum. People who are clinging to the bottom rung of society sit on stoops and lean against lampposts. One woman holds a steaming tin can in a paper napkin as she shovels forkfuls of goop into her drawn face. Her expression suggests that she doesn't know where tomorrow's tinned meal is going to come from.

"Excuse me, can you tell me if there are any cafés around here?" I ask a girl who looks very attractive from behind. She's tall and slim with long, flowing, neatly brushed blond hair.

"What do you want?" she asks, turning to me. Her face is drawn and covered in sores.

"Er, um, I don't mind really, I'm just hungry," I tell her, even though the sensation of hunger has now left me.

"There's a 7-Eleven two blocks up," she says, pointing.

A 7-Eleven you say? How appetizing! As I move away I realize that I am walking in fear. I've quickened my pace, lengthened my stride, trying to bring myself back to my motel, where I wonder about my safety even behind a locked door. Luckily, the motel has a vending machine and I am able to ease my hunger with a pack of Oreos and a Snickers bar. Closing my door behind me, I notice a sign on the inside that reads: FOR YOUR PROTECTION, WHEN IN ROOM ENGAGE DEAD BOLT AND SECURITY LATCH.

What? I am not safe even behind a locked door? I need extra security? A dead bolt? Is there simply no escaping death in the USA? Maybe I have been in Copenhagen too long. Denmark is a small country of only five million people, and therefore all incidents are scaled down in number. We live, for the most part, free of fear and concern.

I turn on the TV and flick through the channels. Surely there is something to occupy my mind? Surely this, the land of entertainment, has something for a scared little Englishman cowering on his dirty little bed.

"They were having a barbecue *on top of the bodies!* I'll tell you what goes through my mind when I hear it, it's called D.P. *DEATH PENALTY!*"

Yes, the land of entertainment does have something for a scared little Englishman: *More death!*

It seems that even before I make it to Neal Smither and the Crime Scene Cleaners I am surrounded by death on all angles. It seems that every way I turn, people are rubbing my nose in death. I am not used to it. It is freaking me out. How on earth can I expect to survive a month with Neal Smither and his Crime Scene Cleaners if I can't even handle the onslaught of death thrown my way by entertainment and strangers on mountainsides?

I find myself presented with a simple choice: I can give myself willingly to the television, knowing that nearly every channel (including most of the cartoon networks) will be pushing death in one form or another, or I can hide my camera and laptop under the bed and once again head out into the real world.

Less concerned than I was earlier, but still walking fast, I head toward the colorful neon lights that adorn bar windows around the world. I buy myself a Corona and place fifty cents on the pool table where two rough-looking Hispanics are playing a game. There aren't many people in this dirty bar, with its barmaid who looks like she was recently sheep-dipped and its walls that are covered in pictures of yesteryear: pictures of a time when the boardwalks were bustling with a holiday crowd. Some of the people in the bar are staring at me and in fairness to them, I do stand out a little. I am the cleanest person in the bar by at least a month.

When it's my turn on the pool table I stroll over and offer a hand to my opponent.

"Hey, I'm Alan."

He shakes my hand but doesn't speak. I rack up; he

breaks. Nothing goes down but the white. I am surprised when I make my first three shots. I feel certain that I will miss soon. But I don't. Instead, I find myself naming the corner pocket for the black, a dead straight shot of about twenty inches. I lie across the table with one leg cocked up on the side and draw the cue back. Happy, because I have never stepped up to a pool table and cleared up before.

"You have to pot the black there!" the Mexican says.

He is pointing to the pocket that's nestling under my crotch. I stand up.

"Why?" I ask.

" 'Cause you mus' pot the black in the opposite pocket to da lass ball you pot. Your lass ball went in dis corner, the black must go in dat corner, or you lose, my friend."

I have never heard of this rule before. But I am still a bit nervous about my surroundings, so I shan't mention that this would have been a nice piece of information to have been furnished with from the outset. Instead, I adjust my angle and actually feel a little relieved at the impossibility of the shot.

I pull the cue back, follow through gently, remove my right leg from the table, and watch as the eight ball comes toward me. Rolling slowly, it disappears into the pocket that the Mexican said I had to aim for. It was a ridiculous shot, one that I couldn't make again in a hundred attempts. It was the kind of shot that could get a stranger beaten up if he was in the wrong bar, in the wrong part of town.

I look at the Mexican with fear in my eyes, and remembering a line from one of my favorite British films, *Withnail and I*, I have the urge to scream, "Please don't hit me, I have cancer: if you hit me it will be murder!"

"What you say your name was?" he asks, looking me in the eye.

"Alan," I croak.

"Hey, Wendy, a beer for my friend Alan! That was good game; where you from?"

"England," I gush with relief.

I am soon engaged in conversation with a crowd of guys at the bar, all of us drinking lots of beer. I am asked why I am in America. I tell them that I'm on my way to San Francisco, to work with a guy who cleans up suicides and homicides.

"He do what?"

The conversation continues for a few minutes in Spanish without me.

"What about da bodies, do . . . are they there?"

As the interest grows and the voices get louder, more and more people come over. If someone's friend enters the bar they are called over to listen to my Neal Smither stories. I tell them stories from my previous visits with Crime Scene Cleaners; I tell them about the scene of the shotgun suicide that Neal took me to last year. They seem genuinely freaked out by the tale. They can't believe that somebody makes his living in this manner.

"He makes a lot of money from this," I tell them.

"I stay poor," a man named Diablo tells me, not living up to his nickname.

The interesting thing about the conversation is that nobody has ever given any thought as to how such bloody scenes get cleaned up. Who cleans up the mess left by the triple homicide that took place in the house across the road? Nobody seems to have an idea. I notice that their grasp of the topic of death has largely been defined by Hollywood. We can imagine all the many and varied ways in which people can die, can be murdered, from the blood squirting from a slit throat to the bloody and charred pulp of a blown-up torso, because we have seen that thousands of times on TV. But we can't imagine how that blood is cleaned from the wall, or how the brain is scooped from the floor, because that part is very rarely, if ever, featured in films and TV dramas. It has not been depicted to us, so we can't begin to imagine it or even accept that somebody real has to clean it up. For the most part, people seem confused about this. *Clean it up?* That stuff doesn't get cleaned up; they just pull the set down and move on to the next film.

Wrong. Death is not a special effect. It does get cleaned up, and across most of America the man behind that cleanup is Neal Smither.

The chitchat in the bar flits from death to death. From Neal to a crash scene somebody's cousin saw a month back, to an uncle who is an EMT and the many war stories he has shared over drinks.

What strikes me from this conversation is that there's a clearly marked line of separation between the average person on the street and those who deal with death on a regular basis. There's an aura, a morbid fascination, around EMTs, firemen, policemen, morticians, and even, in the case of men like Neal Smither, those who clean up the scenes of death. It's as if they have become part of an inner circle, a secret society that lives within the realms of something that for most stifles us with fear. They are respected for their work, but also looked upon with an air of suspicious awe: suspicious because maybe they know something about death that the

31

rest of us don't want to know; maybe they are in league with the dark one. Admire those who work with death, the people in this bar seem to be saying, but do it from afar.

I ran out of money about an hour ago. Having not planned to hang out in a bar all night, I came ill-equipped. As much as I try, however, I appear unable to run out of beer and tequila. That's not entirely true. The tequila in front of me is the same one that was put there forty-five minutes ago and it will remain there until somebody else drinks it. If I were stupid enough to drink it I would be done for. I would later be found in the gutter. Even without the tequila I am swimming in the realms of drunken splendor.

A bunch of the guys, José, Bob, Diablo, and some other guy whose name I can't remember, are leaving. They offer me a ride back to my motel. Foolishly, I find myself getting into the car. As I am squashed in the middle of the backseat, the fear I experienced earlier today comes flooding back.

I am asking myself how I can be so stupid as to be in the back of a car, driven by a drunk Hispanic I've only known for a few hours, sandwiched between some of the dirtiest guys I have ever met, when my motel is just half a mile up the street.

As we wheel-spin from the side of the road I am truly in a state of panic. My throat is tight; my legs feel heavy and my arms weak. The guys all seem different now. Their laughter has turned somehow demonic. I tell myself that I must get out of this. I will fight if I have to. I just know in my heart that fighting won't get me anywhere. I am little match for four guys. I have no heroic notions about my physical abilities. What I have is a rather pathetic yearning to beg for my life.

As the car turns away from the street where my motel is (oh dear God where are they taking me?), I start to consider best- and worst-case scenarios. At this point, scared as I am, I would be happy with a beating. This thought lifts the spirits a bit. *Yeah, a beating's not so bad. I could* live *with a beating.*

After stopping at a liquor store for more booze, the car doubles back and I am dropped off outside my motel. One of the guys, I think Diablo, cries out, "God bless the Queen," as the car screeches off up the road. I scurry back to my room with a light sheen of sweat and panic about me, realizing, as I enter the room, that I left the television on:

> ". . . that trial out of Elkhorn, Wisconsin, of the man who is accused of poisoning his wife. Perhaps you've been following this and would like more detail . . ."

I switch off the TV, aware finally and stupidly of where all my fear came from. Every image that sent me spiraling further into panic—the cars, the demonic laughter, driving in the opposite direction to my motel—they are all scenes lifted from films.

I go to bed knowing that this death business is actually not for me. I have serious concerns about what is going to happen to me when surrounded by real, and not make-believe, death.

DUDE, I'M DYING . . . CHA-CHING!

It's midday by the time I arrive at Neal's house in Orinda, and the neighborhood is peaceful, as was the developer's objective. The street is situated within a golf complex; it is lined with million-dollar houses on either side. Large shiny cars are parked on driveways.

Think sprinklers.

Think Chanel suits.

Think white curbstones with house numbers on them.

Nobody answers when I knock on Neal's door, so I follow the noise of a chainsaw that sounds as though it could be coming from behind the house. As I turn the corner I see a large branch fall from a tree. There's a workman in the garden who collects the branch and feeds it into a shed-size shredder. Neal is at the other end of the garden, with a leaf blower. To his right there's a collection of freshly cut tree stumps.

Strapped to Neal's back is his two-year-old son, Jack,

who appears to be having the time of his life while his father spins around and around. I decide to stay back for a minute. This is a side of Neal that's rarely seen by outsiders.

Neal holds the vacuum hose in the air so that it ruffles Jack's hair. The little boy is waving his arms around and laughing unrestrainedly. I have already met the Neal who celebrates death. It's a relief to see that he puts as much energy into celebrating life.

When he's not speaking in headlines he is clearly a lovable, compassionate fellow. "Hey, Alan buddy. How ya doing?" asks Neal as he notices me leaping away from another falling branch. He shuts down the vacuum. "How's that wife and daughter of yours? You got a picture?"

"Sure," I say, reaching for my wallet.

"Wow, she looks just like her mama, huh? That's some big beautiful eyes she's got there." Neal's cell phone rings. "Crime Scene Cleaners, Neal speaking, how may I help you?" There's a pause as the caller makes an inquiry. "Okay, let me ask you some questions, that way you don't have to explain everything to me and feel it. Gunshot or knife?"

Jack, still strapped to Neal's back, looks out into the garden, waving his hands around and talking to himself. He's a very happy boy; his expression tells me that there's no place he'd rather be right now than strapped to his dad's back.

"Shotgun, that's all I needed to know. Let me explain our services to you. We would send someone out; if you like the estimate, they'd do the job immediately. Everything is guaranteed and one price is gonna fix the whole thing. So one price will clean it, disinfect it, deodorize it, and dispose of the waste. Averages for us: three hundred bucks for something pretty simple, to a nightmare shotgun suicide which you can pretty much guarantee is gonna be right about two thousand to twenty-five hundred bucks max, okay? What I recommend is get us in there and let us look at it, it doesn't cost you a dime. Okay, Lisa, gotcha." Neal's expression hardens as the call takes an unexpected turn. "Yes, ma'am, if he moved around and made a mess that's fine, we'll clean it even if it's in three rooms; one person can only make a certain amount of mess. So don't worry . . . It's two people? . . . In two separate rooms? I'm going to come and take care of you myself. I'm on my way."

Neal runs into the house and picks up a notepad from the kitchen table and starts taking directions. He has half a smile unfurling across his face. "Double shotgun suicide, San Francisco!" he cries in delight. "How d'you like that, buddy? You walk through my door and I get you a job straight away, a good one, too, by the sounds of it. Tell me I'm not the man!" Neal jogs around the house exuberantly, looking for his wife.

As you might expect, Neal's house is clean, sanitary even. There's nothing out of place in the kitchen, no dishes waiting to be loaded into the dishwasher and no crumbs on the counter. There are no magazines on the floor in the living room. No TV remotes protruding from between sofa cushions. On the shelves all around the living room are crime-fiction hardbacks. There appears to be just about everything from John Grisham and P. D. James to James Ellroy. You could dust them if you wanted to, but I doubt you'd find a single fingerprint, that's how clean this place is. I realize that I am not supposed to be in here with my shoes on.

"Lyndey? Lyndey? Oh, there you are. Gotta go, baby. Alan, come on, let's go!"

As the truck pulls away I am pinned firmly into my seat. The inside of the truck (I kid you not) is bigger than the bathroom in my apartment back home. It is like a luxury penthouse with its leather seats and its air conditioning. Neal pops a CD in the stereo and turns it up. The truck is filled with the sounds of the Harlem Gospel Choir. The music is in such stark contrast to Neal's character that I can't help but giggle.

"*Dude,* what the fuuuuck? You should hear the voices on these motherfuckers, man! CD only came out last week," he says, as if to show me that he is always up-to-date with the gospel scene.

As we speed up the on-ramp and onto the interstate, Neal's phone rings and the Harlem Gospel Choir is temporarily muted.

"Crime Scene Cleaners. Okay, ma'am, just stay on the line. I'm gonna get my guy on the radio and see where he is. Hold on." Neal opens a compartment between the seats in his truck as he swerves down another ramp to Interstate 560; he removes another cell phone from a compartment between the seats and dials a number. "Where are you, Shawn? The customer's waiting. Well, listen, get a move on. I don't want this woman calling me to ask where you are, got it? "

The truck eases up to ninety miles per hour. Neal has one cell phone held to his left ear and another held to his right. He is taking directions from one and giving them to the other. The dusty landscape blurs past as the truck, minus the aid of hands, barrels along the highway. You would think that if you were going to drive without the employment of either hand you would slow down and stay in lane. But Neal presses the gas pedal down and uses his knees to steer as he cuts into another lane and starts overtaking cars. It could be a skill he developed while playing Atari Space Invaders in the 1980s, where the options were limited to moving only left or right. That's pretty much how Neal handles things. He ignores the ninety miles per hour of forward motion and simply concentrates on moving left and right whenever the traffic pattern requires it.

We pass a huge silver SUV in the inside lane. There's a middle-aged woman driving. Sitting next to her in the passenger seat is a girl who must be her teenage daughter. The mother, if that's what she is, looks over and immediately gasps in horror. In slow motion her mouth forms the words "*Oh my God!*", causing her daughter to look over. She also gasps and mouths the words "*Oh my God!*" She pushes her sunglasses down on her nose and I know what's coming next. Her mouth forms the words "*Crime Scene Cleaners*" as she reads the sign on the door. "*Homicide, Suicide and—Oh my God!*" The two women look so horrified that I wonder how on earth they are going to recover from the spectacle of Neal overtaking them at what is now ninety-five miles per hour without holding on to the steering wheel.

Slowly they fall behind us.

This is not my first experience with Neal's no-handed kamikaze routine. Having learned something from my first encounter with Neal, I try to sit still. I concentrate on not letting any little gasps escape from my mouth, knowing that for every gasp the speed will increase another two miles per hour. Neal is a master tormentor, so I try to act nonchalant. I slide my right arm up on the door and slouch down in my seat. I fidget nonchalantly with my mobile phone. Then we nearly impact with a car that's driving as stupidly as we are and I jump out of my skin screaming.

"Aaaarrrh!"

The seat belt garrotes the right side of my neck as, for reasons inexplicable to me, I try to climb through the roof. The truck cuts left at an oblique angle.

"What are you doing?" Neal asks me in a tranquil voice. He is no longer talking on either of the phones and has both hands firmly on the wheel. "You've got to do something about that, Alan, jeez. You're gonna hurt yourself one of these days."

Just like the first time I met Neal, I fall into a state of regret. Not because of his persona: I am already aware of his shock tactics. It's just that I don't want to die, and being in a car with Neal increases my chances of death a thousand-fold. If my life insurance broker could see me now (if I had one, that is) he would cancel my policy and give me my money back.

When we arrive at the murder/suicide, Neal is not, as I am, openmouthed by all the theater. There are several squad cars parked up with their lights flashing. Long strips of yellow tape flutter in the light breeze, informing us that this is indeed a crime scene and that we should stay away and mind our own business.

Police officers stand about drinking coffee. Neighbors look out from behind curtains; some stand on the pavement directly outside the house, bugging the police officers for details. *How much blood was there? What kind of gun was it? Which rooms are the bodies in?* Everybody on the scene wants a little bit of tragedy to take home with them, a bloody tale to save until the right moment presents itself. Like maybe in a bar to a gaggle of drunken strangers whom you want to impress, just like I did in Santa Cruz. I guess for those of us who lead a normal and for the most part uneventful life, stories, especially those that make people around a table sit up and listen, are what we're defined by. Stories serve an incredible purpose. They fill voids and lighten awkward moments. They bridge gaps between strangers and build status among friends. You don't need to be a novelist, but if you have enough content and delivery to hold people's attention for five minutes you will be invited to the next barbecue, because a good story well told makes us, vicariously, more interesting.

Stories of death work well. The majority of people have a strong sense of morbid intrigue running through them. Morbid intrigue produces, among other things, rubberneckers on the highway—those who crane and twist their necks as they cruise past a five-car pileup. Sure, we swear at them when we sit in the ten-mile traffic jam they cause, but do we listen to their stories as they are told around the coffee machine at the next sales meeting, in the bar between plays on the big screen, around the grill while we flip burgers? You betcha!

Feel free to test it. Go into work tomorrow and tell your colleagues that a neighbor shot his wife with a shotgun and then turned it on himself. Tell them about all the flashing lights and hoo-hah, about how nice your neighbors had seemed. I'll wager the contents of my apartment that it will be one of your most popular mornings in the office. Because the story of dead neighbors is much more interesting than what was on TV last night, or what you had for dinner, or the fact that the monthly sales are down, or up, or wherever they may be.

The people on the street now, badgering the police and trying desperately to get a glimpse of something, will enjoy some popularity for days to come. They'll go to bed tonight with the story formulating in their minds and wake up tomorrow with it spilling out of their mouths.

Some of the officers, mostly the older ones, are irritated by this crowd, but some seem to enjoy the questions. They, right now, hold the story. The answers. They are inside the circle and enjoy the status it brings them.

"Hey, Crime Scene Cleaners are here!" an officer calls out with a flick of the head and a big grin as Neal and I approach the tape. The officer lifts the tape for us to stoop under. He's glad to see Neal. "Hey, buddy, I wondered when you'd be along. It's a messy one," he says as Neal signs us into the scene. Neal knows most of the officers in the San Francisco Bay Area. What with them chasing death and Neal cleaning up after death, their paths cross regularly.

"What we got?" Neal asks.

"Murder/suicide . . ." the officer begins.

"Nice."

"Dude offed his old lady in the living room with a double barrel, then went in the bedroom, reloaded, and put the barrels in his own mouth. . . . BOOM!"

"Nice."

"Yep. It's a pretty sad story, though. She was suffering from some illness. I guess he couldn't watch it anymore. You can go straight in."

"Okay, boss! I'll go suit up."

Neal walks back to the truck, unlocks a steel box in the back, and removes two blue protective suits, one for each of us. We also put on breathing masks and protective gloves before grabbing a workbox, a twelve-pack of industrial tissue, and a tank of enzyme that has been specially produced for the very job of breaking down blood.

We then head back over to the house, our nylon protective suits rustling as we walk. I feel a little mad dressed like this. We are not chemical experts, but it feels like that.

Clad in the suits and the masks, we get a lot of attention. People look at us as if to say: "Wow, they're going in." It feels funny, to be the center of people's fascination. By wearing the gear, I am, at least from a distance, inside the dark circle. It's unsettling, feeling the eyes that follow us all the way through the door; I feel a little creeped out.

"Whoops!" Neal shouts through his mask as we enter the bloody bedroom and survey the scene. Very quickly I am brought back to reality, away from the sensation of being slightly interesting to the people outside. I am not, I realize with a startled spine, even close to being inside the dark circle.

I stand stiff-limbed and dry-mouthed as I stare at the walls and ceiling: it looks like they have been spray-painted with blood and brain.

I am aware of Neal moving around the room, checking out how messy the furniture is (deciding whether it should be cleaned or thrown), but at the same time I am not really aware. My brain registers Neal's movement, but seems incapable of initiating any of my own. I stand inert. This is beyond anything that I saw in my previous trips with Neal. I am becoming short of breath as my eyes flick around in disbelief. My mind is caught up in a rhythmic chanting: *No this can't be. No this can't be. No this can't be.*

Pieces of brain, I can't help but notice, are literally clinging to the plaster like pink limpets. Some have left streaks on the bloody wall where they have slid down. Others, having impacted the wall at great speed, are stuck fast.

A piece of skull fragment has positioned itself on the bedside cabinet next to a glass of water. The skull piece looks like it was always there, like a ceramic memento brought back from a holiday in Greece. The glass of water now looks like a strawberry daiquiri. Half a jawbone lies discarded on the floor next to the bed.

The smell actually isn't all that bad. Shotgun suicides make a lot of noise, which normally means that they are found straightaway, before decomposition sets in. The odor is sweet; you can feel the stickiness as it tries to worm its way down the esophagus.

"Oh yeah, you can see where he did this, right on the bed," begins Neal, after finishing his examination of the room. "You see the spray on the window and the ceiling? The angle of the spray basically tells you where he was sitting. The stuff all over the wall there, that's exactly what you think it is—his brains. Well, his brain matter anyway. Oh yeah, this is a funky one."

I follow Neal as he walks through the hallway, leaving his bloody footprints mingled with those left behind by the police. He enters the dining room, stepping aside as the body bag is carried past him.

"Motherfucker! This *is* a messy one. I gotta get backup." Neal unzips his suit and rummages for his cell phone.

"Hey, Steve, guess what . . . Yeah, sorry, dude, I know it's your day off. You need to stop off and pick up more supplies. . . . Yeah, of everything." Neal gives the address and hangs up.

There is little tomfoolery when Neal starts working. He moves swiftly, aware that the clock is ticking and ahead of him lies protracted toil. Etiquette tells me that I should offer to help. I don't feel comfortable standing around watching other people work, especially when they are doing a labor-intensive job on their own. But I don't want this under my fingernails. I am here to document, not to get my hands bloody. I try to blend in with the background.

Neal starts by removing the big blood-contaminated items first. Working from the bedroom, he covers the mattress in a large plastic sheet and tapes it up, being sure not to leave any gaps from which blood can seep out.

"Alan, get the other end of this," he says, without much of a glance in my direction. I look back incredulously and am about to speak when he cuts me off. "Oh, don't be a pussy, just grab the other fucking end of the mattress. You don't even have any of the gore. I've got the gore at my end."

The mattress is several pounds heavier than it ought to be on account of all the blood it has soaked up, which makes me instantly aware of just how sedentary my life as a journalist has been. For a second I forget where I am and what I'm doing and have to question when was the last time I picked up anything heavier than my daughter. But I am brought back to the room by the sight of blood seeping along the plastic from Neal's end of the mattress to mine. I can actually hear the blood trickling toward me. Sure, it's inside the plastic wrapping, but it's still coming my way.

After carrying out the mattress, I go back to the bed-room and take the bloodstained bedclothes, roll them into a ball, and place them in a black garbage bag, which I then throw into the back of the truck. Neal is going through the contents of drawers. Everything is removed cautiously to make sure that nothing picks up any blood on the way. The items are put into thick, heavy-duty trash bags, which are then carried away to an uncontaminated room. Later, rela-tives will go through the possessions, but right now they are in the way.

A couple of other trucks arrive. They also have the Crime Scene Cleaners logo written on the side, the only dif-ference being that these trucks are white. It seems there's a similar hierarchy in Crime Scene Cleaners to that of the *Star Wars* movies. Neal, in his big black truck, moves around like the Dark Lord. His minions are in white.

Some of the guys who have arrived had been working on another suicide thirty minutes away. They are here to help remove the contaminated furniture and take it straight to a biohazard landfill before they return to their own mess. Neal starts issuing commands.

"Okay, you start bringing out all the furniture from the bedroom, load it on this truck. Jake, I've tied all this shit on my truck down, it's all secure, so you can take my truck now, dump it and haul ass back here. Don't fuck around, I want you back here fast. If you get pulled over for speeding, tell them that you are doing a job for the county sheriff's de-partment, tell them to get on the radio."

In no time at all the second truck is half loaded, leaving the bedroom empty and ready for a chemical attack. The only other thing left in the room is the carpet, which is left down while the cleaning continues. This way it can catch all the sediment as it is scraped off the walls and ceiling.

"Hey, Alan, come here. Can you see these dinks in the back house over there? Look at that, the whole fucking family up at the window watching," Neal says, pointing out the window; and indeed an entire family are craning their necks and pushing one another aside in a bid to get a better view. "Freaky fucks!" Neal shouts. "If only you'd been this interested when they were alive, motherfuckers!"

Neal starts scraping the brain from the wall.

"Brain," Neal tells me in a didactic tone, "dries quickly, like cement. So it's real easy to deal with."

For this job Neal uses a putty knife that gets under sediment easily. Essentially, he wants to get the walls to a state where they are only stained, which also means removing the skull fragments that have been stuck fast in the wall.

"The problem with skull fragment, Alan, is it gets everywhere. You see little pieces like this?" Neal wipes pink matter from a small piece of skull that's about the size of a baby's tooth. "This shit gets everywhere. If the door to this room was open when he shot her, or himself, whichever way it was, there's gonna be pieces of skull out there in the hallway. That shit hits the wall at three hundred feet per second, so the bits that don't get lodged bounce a long fucking way, dude. You wouldn't believe some of the places I've found skull fragments."

I decide to test this bounce theory of Neal's. Not because I don't believe him, but because I don't, regardless of how dry it may be, want to scrape brain from the wall. I don't want to pick pieces of skull from the plaster walls with my rubber-gloved fingers the way Neal does.

"Gotcha . . . Gotcha . . . Gotcha . . ."

I head out to the hallway, where the carpet, which used to be light green, is now heavily soiled with bloody footprints from all the coming and going. Some of the footprints, I realize with a shudder, are mine. I am surprised at the mess. Surprised on one level that so many people have been through here. Surprised on another that it isn't a restricted area. But then I guess there wasn't much need to preserve the crime scene. They may run some powder tests on the guy's clothing to make sure he fired the gun, but from the scene investigation the police have extrapolated that this is a cut-and-dried case. They have no reason to concern themselves with traipsing bloody footprints, reminiscent of something you might expect to see in a horror film, through the house.

There are no obvious skull pieces on the hallway carpet. I crouch down for closer inspection but still I see no proof of Neal's bounce theory.

"You see any?" Neal calls out.

"Nah."

"Keep looking!"

I begin to sweep my foot over the carpet. Nothing. Nothing. Nothing. Ooh, what's that? Something flicked up, but I've lost it again. Nothing. Nothing. There it is. But it's too white to be skull, there's no blood on it. It's probably . . .

"What about this?" I proudly show Neal my finding as I walk back into the bedroom.

"Tooth! Dude, that's a fucking white tooth, too. Bitch took care a those."

Neal's harshness sends a shudder down my back. What am I doing? Why, in this poignant, melancholy scene, am I playing hide-and-seek with skull fragments and teeth? I am surrounded by exploded head. Blood and gore line every wall. It's not as if it's easy to forget where I am or what took place here. How then is it so easy to ignore the tragedy? Neal has had years of exposure to this kind of thing; his job has hardened him, turned off certain sensors. I, on the other hand, have no such justification. This should be an absolute horror to me, not an experience. What incident happened in my life to turn off my sensors? There has been no such episode; I have had no such exposure. Yet, here I stand, and it's all so familiar. I've been here before. All this mess, it's blood in a can, it's directed by Quentin Tarantino. The shotgun-perforated head is, after all, one of the most successfully and repeatedly used pillars of the entertainment industry. So, while I may have frozen upon entry, it very quickly became something surreal. Like an out-of-body experience, it all looks so familiar, but at the same time I feel disconnected from it.

Neal, on the other hand, is going about his work as if he were a calm and happy postman enjoying the first days of spring. For a long time he is whistling, but after a while, so overjoyed is he, he breaks into song. The words are unfamiliar to me, I think it may be something he composed himself.

"You are dead . . . motherfucker
You are dead . . . motherfucker
You are dead . . . motherfucker
I am not . . ."

The skull pieces, teeth, and jawbone are discarded into a regular trash bag like regular trash. I guess there's no reason why they shouldn't be, but as well as being a harsh reality it is very depressing to observe.

"These are the ones that make you feel bad," Neal reflects over the sound of scraping. "They really do. Did you see the photographs in the other room? I mean these people were in their late seventies or eighties. From what the officer told me, the wife was in late-stages Alzheimer's and the husband just couldn't take care of her anymore is what it amounted to. You know, they've probably been together their whole lives and he didn't want to give up. So they had made a pact. You know, when she got to a certain stage he's gonna kill her. And that's what he did: he blew her brains out in the living room and then came in the bedroom and blew his own brains out. You know, I don't know if they so much affect me, but these are the ones I have sympathy for, as opposed to Johnny Dirtbag who's blown his brains out to tell mom and dad 'Fuck you!' because he had his car taken away for the weekend."

"Do you think about it a lot while you work?"

"No. Not typically. Not anymore. I just think about what I'm doing, make sure I do a good job."

Steve is emptying the drawers of the bloodstained cabinets in the living room. He is looking for legal documents such as wills, bank statements, or deeds. If he finds any such documents, they will be filed in a box and handed over to the relatives later. Everything else is to be discarded.

Cleaning bloodstains off walls can be long, hard work. Neal works on sections that are two feet square. With a stiff brush and a chemical enzyme, he scrubs hard in a circular motion. It's not like a detergent commercial that you might see on TV; the blood doesn't come off in one white-toothed sing-along swipe. Quite the contrary. The work is tough and the results of the hard, incessant scrubbing come slowly. The enzyme that Neal uses is a mixture of ingredients that have been blended to break down blood without eating into the surface that it sits on. It makes things slower, but it means that Neal doesn't cause as much damage as he repairs. Once the enzyme has liquefied the blood, he wipes it up with industrial tissue that he goes through at an expeditious rate.

"Enamel-based paint is the best surface for cleaning blood from a wall. It wipes up real easy. But with a textured wall you have to play with the blood a little more. You have to be gentler 'cause you don't wanna take the texture off the wall; you don't wanna remove the paint. It's really just a matter of learning how each wall surface is gonna react to your enzyme. So what I do is I apply it in a mist and attack a small area. I wipe it up and look at the wall; if it needs repeating I repeat it. When I'm doing a wall I always attack small areas, small sections at a time, maybe two feet by three feet max. That way, if my enzyme isn't working well with the wall finish, I haven't ruined a six-foot square of wall. In this game we have to guarantee everything. It's body fluid, so mom and dad are already, you know, extremely skeptical. There's a lot of salesmanship involved, but you still have to do a good job. It's the ceiling that really pisses people off, or where you might find the bad work if it's a new guy working for you, 'cause the arms just start hurting immediately if you're not used to working with your arms above your head. Right off the bat I can tell a lot about a new worker by checking the quality of the ceiling after he's cleaned it. I can tell from that if they're just freaks who wanna tell their friends they are crime scene cleaners, or if they have some pride, both personally, but also . . . You know, the thing is, if it's a kid who's killed themselves, mom and pop don't wanna move a plant to one side a month down the line only to find a missed blood splatter. I mean that's just not on. And that's partly what I do—I play a game with it, I simply will not leave a speck behind for the parents, or loved ones or whoever, to find."

Neal seems to work even harder on the ceilings. It's as if he is angry. He wants this part of the job to be over ASAP so that he can get his own blood back into his arms.

"I could use a smoke right now," he tells me as he works away. "What I used to do on jobs like this is I would tell myself that I can't have a smoke until the walls and ceiling are free of brain and sediment and are wiped and clean of any bloodstains. Otherwise I'd be taking a smoke break every five minutes and this job would take twice as long. I quit smoking six months ago, but I still think about it that way; I still pretend I'm gonna have a cigarette break after a certain amount of work."

Somehow, that is typical of Neal. The very things that would drive others crazy, or at least have them running for the nearest pack of cigarettes, actually drive Neal on in the direction of his choosing.

Finally, after several hours of scrubbing, Neal stands outside the house, shouting into his cell phone, "Come on, asshole, I don't wanna be here all night! Jeeeesus!"

He's waiting for Steve to get back from the landfill so that they can start emptying the dining room.

For somebody with little esteem for the dead, it's amazing to see how much respect Neal has for the property that they leave behind. In the bedroom, he gently eases the baseboard from the wall with a hammer and a screwdriver, being careful not to leave marks in the wall. He works as much with his ears as his hands, as he listens for the sound of the wood splintering, easing off a little whenever he does. He peers behind the baseboard, looking for the nails so that he can get right in behind them, limiting the chances of breaking the baseboard.

"Do you always remove the baseboards?" I ask.

"Generally we only pull the baseboard out if liquid has gone underneath, 'cause there's no way to just clean behind it if you don't pull it. It'll just keep leaking out from under there. Like, maybe not now, but you'll get a real hot day and if there's stuff behind it could leak out; it would smell a bit, too, I imagine. Usually, how it breaks down is that, if it seems like they can't afford to replace the baseboard, we clean it. If they can afford to replace it, then it's coming with us. My job is not to sit there for hours on end cleaning the baseboards. But you know, for some people money is that tight and so we do what we can, when and if we can. If it's ten P.M. and there's another three jobs waiting to be done that baseboard is coming up and I couldn't give a shit how many pieces it breaks into. But like, here I gotta wait for the other truck to get here before I can start on the other room, so I have the time."

Together we go about pulling the carpet up, starting on one side and rolling it back across the room. It's heavy and does not come easy. About a quarter of the carpet is stained. Underneath the blood has seeped out, gone through the foam pad, and stained at least half the floor. At this point, a family member enters the house to see how the job is coming along.

"Oh wow! You really get it this clean?" he says. "Hi, I'm Dave. You spoke to my wife on the phone."

"Hi, Dave. Neal Smither, Crime Scene Cleaners. Yeah . . . Well, I'm not done yet. You can't get bloodstains out of floorboards. That's soaked in there and it ain't coming out. But what I do is I scrub it clean, disinfect it, and then paint a sealant over it, so you won't be able to see the stain and it's of no danger. It's clean and sealed, and it can't rot the floor or anything like that."

"And the other room?" asks Dave.

"Yeah." Neal pauses. "Don't go in there. We're about to start the initial cleanup. It's been emptied, the paperwork has been filed like we were asked, but it's still a big mess."

"Okay, well, when should I come back, 'cause I gotta write you a check for this on completion, right?"

"Oh yes, you do. About four hours I'd say, but you can just call me and make sure we're done or I'll call you."

"Okay, well, give me a call."

I start taping black bags over the ends of the carpet so that no fragments can fall out when it is moved. I also split a couple of bags and tape them around the middle. Neal and I carry the carpet out to his now empty truck.

"You're damn straight you gotta pay me on completion, *damn*. I don't know why you're asking me, I made it very clear on the phone," Neal says to himself.

"Do you have much trouble with people paying?"

"Used to. When we would send the invoice in the mail, people would be like, 'How much? All he did was clean.' You know, most of the time the invoice would go to someone who didn't see the mess before we cleaned it, so they see the invoice for a couple of grand and they're like, 'Get outta here.' Now I don't give them any time to think. In the here-and-now, people will pay you a lot of money to clean up dead bodies. They don't want to touch what we touch, but you need to get that money at the time or else . . . Not all of them, though."

"Have you ever had somebody try to not pay you at the end of a job?"

"Hell yeah!"

"What did you do about that?"

"I went out to my truck, unroped it, dragged that big, bloody, fluid-filled mattress back in there. I got the bedclothes and they were just off the fucking chart; if I remember right, it was a decomp. Grandpa died in his bed and his shitty kids didn't find him for like a month. This was in July, so it was hot. I mean we're talking strong odors. We're talking maggots. I ripped open those plastic bags and just threw the shit back in the room."

"What was the guy saying? Was it a guy?"

"Yeah, it was a guy. He was like, 'You can't do that.' I said, 'Listen, you fucking dink, you knew the deal: I clean, you pay. You don't pay, I dump the shit back.' You see, he thought, 'Oh yeah, I'll get this guy to clean, then I won't pay. What can he do once he's cleaned—unclean it?' And I'm like, 'Fuck yeah! That's exactly what I can do!' So then he tried to backtrack and wanted to pay me half. I was like, 'Fuck you. Keep your money. I don't need it.' But generally, people are shocked when we leave. Extremely happy—extremely happy and extremely shocked and I guess dismayed that they're having to have this done to begin with. There are just so many emotions involved."

The scrubbing and disinfecting of the bedroom floor takes no time at all. Neal leaves it to dry and will seal it as one of his last jobs. He heads into the living room and starts all over again.

"Some of them are just much sadder than others. I don't really get involved in that part of it anymore, 'cause frankly I don't care. You guys wanna live like that and blow each other away? Fucking A. Go for it. Just leave my card where your relatives will find it! But every now and then you'll get one where you think, '*God Almighty*! How do these people do that to each other?'

"Another sad one that I did a while back—and this made world news, actually—was a sausage producer in the Bay Area, a sausage-making factory. His facilities probably weren't as clean as they should've been, so the inspectors were, you know, fighting the hell outta him, making him clean his place. And he finally couldn't take it anymore and so the next time they came in he was ready for them. He shot three of them dead and just wounded the other two. So when we get there, you know, he's in jail, he's gonna go to death row, or actually he's on death row right now. But his ninety-two-year-old mother, who had just lost another kid due to cancer, is now stuck with a kid who's on death row and this sausage factory. So she's gotta take care of his business, she's gotta take care of the police, she's gotta take care of the federal inspectors, the press, the cleaners; plus her son is on death row. So at ninety-two years old she has to take care of his screwup. You know, those are pretty disgusting."

"Do you get angry about things like that?"

"Yeah, I get angry! But what can you do? I mean, it's not your family. It's not your business. You're there to clean the mess and get out. It's just sad. Those kinds of things are just sad."

After another hour or so, the room is looking well on its way to being clean. Two more of Neal's minions in white trucks return from another finished job.

"Okay, boys, one of you has got to go empty my truck at the dump for me. Who's it gonna be? Shall we flip for it?"

"Nah, man, I can't: I gotta date," one of them says.

"I'll do it," says the other. "But you owe me next time one of us has to do a late."

"Are you taking flowers?" Neal asks.

"Nah, man, it's only a date."

"Do you wanna take her this?" Neal asks, holding out a piece of skull. It's about the size of a small hand. "You can tell her it's an ashtray. Tell her you made it for her at night school. I'll clean the brain off? Or you could just take it home and have your morning cereal out of it?"

Everybody in the room is laughing.

"I'll stay and help here for, like, thirty minutes, if you want?"

"Nah, you've got a date, go get cleaned up. Don't forget to wash behind your ears. Where you taking her?" Neal asks him.

There's a good vibe in the room, the vibe of four young people laughing and joking with one another, discussing dates and good restaurants. It's as if all the people in the room are immune to the fact of death.

"The guy at the landfill is gonna piss his pants when he sees me again," the cleaner who is about to drive away with a loaded truck says with a laugh. "This is like the fifth time today."

"You should always make friends with dump people," says Neal earnestly, " 'cause if they lock us out, we're fucked. You just gotta make friends with them. If they don't like you, you're not getting shit done and I mean nothing. Realistically, they have more clout than the governing agencies."

Three hours later, the rooms are clean and checked. Even the hallway, which had blood splatters all the way from the living room, has been cleaned and checked three times. All bloodstains have been eradicated. There are little pit marks here and there in the walls and ceilings, but the skull pieces and flying teeth that caused them have all been scraped, scooped, and bagged. The air is pungent with the smell of chemicals, like the sealant that's still wet on the floors, or the deodorizer that's been sprayed in the air. It doesn't smell good, but it doesn't smell of fatality, either.

As Neal waits for the relative to arrive with the check, the phone rings and gets picked up by the answering machine.

"Hey, Dan, it's Doug. Just calling to see if we're still meeting this weekend. Give me a call."

There's a loud plastic *click* as the machine starts winding the tape back into position.

"I'm sorry," Neal's voice begins. "We can't come to the phone right now 'cause we're dead. Feel free to leave a message, but if we don't get back to you, it's because we're dead. Have a nice day now."

"Neal, for God's sake!" I say.

"Whaaaat? Oh, here's our man with the check. Let's go."

I collect my car and follow Neal to a Motel 6 in a place called Walnut Creek, which is between the town where Neal lives and the town where he has his office. It is nicely situated for me to hit the road at a second's notice.

The motel room is dull—just like any room in any national motel chain anywhere in the world. But it is clean. In fact, it's like a palace compared to the place I stayed in Santa Cruz. There's no unpacking my suitcase, no getting undressed or even cleaning my teeth. I lie on the bed flicking through TV channels, but before anything takes my fancy I'm fast asleep.

I am a fantasist. There's no escaping it. It's a pastime that has followed me energetically from childhood into adulthood. Here I am in my thirties and still incapable of watching an action movie without a small part of me fantasizing myself as a liberating hero. I am the longest-running James Bond ever. I get the gun, I get the car, I get the girl, and I get them several times over and in many and varied ways.

But oddly I don't want to be a hero in everyday life. In that, I have no interest. Because, quite frankly, where does one find the time? Being a hero is highly inconvenient to personal schedules and needs.

For example, right now I am sitting outside a Mexican restaurant in Walnut Creek. My table is up against a waist-high metal railing that separates the restaurant from the sidewalk. I am reading a book, pending the imminent arrival of chicken fajitas, when I am rudely interrupted by a crunching thud.

Hmmm, I think to myself. *Curious*. But I am at a good part in the book (*Down and Out in Paris and London*, George Orwell on poverty) and so I continue to read without looking. As good as the book is, however, I find myself unable to ignore the fact that this crunch took place right next to me, practically at my feet.

And so of course I have to take a look.

On the other side of the railing lies a body, facedown and lifeless. I hear a chorus of gasps and recognize them as shock and horror.

I turn the page of my book and continue reading.

It's not that I'm a total asshole. It's just, well, I'm just not buying what they are selling. It looks like a lot of drama to me. The cries of "oh my GOD!" just seem like so much bad acting, like canned concern. I don't want any part of it. The body next to me will no doubt stand up in a minute or so, feel embarrassed, but all the same dust off the pants and scuttle off as quickly as possible.

And so I read on.

"Mom?" I hear.

"Mom?" again.

"Are you okay? Mom?"

I have been brought up with manners, believe it or not. I shouldn't sit here reading. I know this, of course. And given that the daughter is genuinely starting to panic and the body—the mother—continues to lie limp on the ground, I shall rise and see if I can be of assistance. But I am too late, there's already a cooperative of males circling the drama. No more than a few seconds have passed since the initial crunch, but in that time many men have sprung into action. So I decide not to rise. I have no first-aid skills, I have nothing extra to offer, and there are now several people gathered at the scene. So, I once more give a quick, cursory glance to see if there is any chance of the waitress arriving with my fajitas anytime soon, and return once again to my book.

But, again, I am distracted as something blurs past me. Is it a bird? Is it a plane? No! It's the guy who *was* sitting three tables back, tie flapping in the wind as he bounds the railing. He even looks a little like Clark Kent, and while his tie may have been flapping, his hair, let me tell you, is steadfast.

There are already several men on the scene, but this does not stop our man. He knows in his heart of hearts that he is the chap for the job and thus asserts his authority without delay.

"Stand back, make space . . ."

"Are you a doctor?" somebody asks.

"Please," our man insists. "Will you stand back!"

"Are you a doctor?" somebody asks again.

"No," our man finally relents. "But I'm going to need some space here."

I totally agree with him. I mean, it seems like the smartest move, right? Yes, that's it, clear a big circle so that everybody can see you at the center of it. The fact that the body, a rather well-dressed woman lying facedown at my feet, is still not moving seems to have eluded all, except the daughter, who is frantically hopping and pleading with her mother to respond.

Even I am a little concerned now.

However, I remain ill-mannered. I am ill-mannered because the woman's needs are secondary to my not wanting to enter a pissing contest. The other men leaping around are ill-mannered because the woman's needs are secondary to their *wanting* to take part in a pissing contest.

To my surprise, not a single woman has risen to the occasion. The female participation in this tragedy is purely of the seated variety. They call out encouragement from their tables:

"Is she okay?"

"Is she moving?"

"Did she hit her head?"

"It was a nasty fall!"

The women are ill-mannered for sitting back and letting their incompetent men quantify their limp penises while a woman lies on the floor in need of aid.

The men continue to dance around.

"Stand *back*, please!"

The lady is still not moving.

But I am confident that one of the men will establish himself as this scene's protagonist and come to the damsel's aid. I am convinced of it and so I watch on while two men team up and hunker down together, one guy resigning himself to the role of sidekick.

"Check her pulse!" Batman says to Robin.

"Where should I check it, the wrist or the neck?"

"I don't think it matters . . . *the wrist.*"

I have had enough of this. I *am* going to seize control. I am the protagonist here, the reluctant hero, which makes me more heroic. I pick up my mobile phone and with my bionic thumb and my Newton-like grasp of numbers I dial 911. Yes, I am Thumb Man. Never before has a button been so pressed. My gallant thumbs are legendary; many a situation have they saved.

"Can you just give me a second to breathe?" the body at my feet says, still not moving but giving a clear sign of being.

And that is pretty much that. She rolls over and with assistance from too many men clambers to her feet. I stand and pick up my chair, holding it over the railing for somebody to take, but our man from three tables back, The Blur, decides that my chair is not worthy enough. With another puff of the chest he leaps the railing, selects another chair, ignores the many arms reaching out to take it from him, and leaps back over the railing and places the chair on the sidewalk.

The lady appears to be more afflicted with embarrassment than anything else. Her daughter is laughing in sheer relief and the men are loitering, not wanting to leave the damsel's side. But soon enough they are on their way—no blood spilled, just a six-dollar frappuccino. The extent of the injury: a sprained ankle—a badly sprained ankle, I have no doubt, but a sprained ankle nonetheless. The lady hobbles off, leaning on her daughter. Her car, she assures everybody listening, is just around the corner; her daughter will drive.

And so the men disband.

Those who were enjoying dinner come back to their tables; others continue on their way. And just as soon as the sidewalk is clear of any evidence that there ever was a situation, my ambulance, with red lights ablaze, a burst of siren, and a screech of tire, skids to a halt outside the restaurant.

As they look up and down the sidewalk for the unconscious woman they had been told about, the EMTs look somewhat confused. But what's interesting is that nobody, and I include myself, says a word to them. Every single person outside the Mexican restaurant ignores the EMTs as they pace up and down.

But then one of them notices the puddle of spilled coffee and walks over in my direction.

"Was it you that called an ambulance?" he asks me.

"Yes—but she's gone now, it wasn't as bad as—"

"What do you mean she's gone? You reported her as unconscious."

"Well, she looked like she was, but then . . . *she wasn't.*" I look around, expecting somebody to back me up, but fail miserably to meet even a single pair of eyes.

"Well, how did she leave?" the EMT annoyingly persists.

"On foot," I tell him. "She was limping, though!" I offer as proof that there had been some gravity to the scene, that she hadn't got away with the fraud scot-free. Still, nobody else around me—none of the heroes—speaks up to explain that the lady on the ground really had looked insentient. Not one person backs me up when I say that she wasn't moving, that she showed little sign of life. For I am a man: I am not worthy of another man's assistance. There is no glory in assisting me with my elucidation. And thus, I decide with some finality as I once again look longingly for the arrival of my fajitas, the competitive world of the male superhero is a world in which I will no longer roam. The next person who needs my bionic thumbs will lie there limp for a week! Unless, of course, they make a bloody mess, and then I will call Neal Smither, who is starting to look with every passing day more like a real-life hero than anybody I have ever met.

If we look at the classic American hero, Neal fits the bill perfectly. He is an outsider, for starters, not just in his line of work but in his character. He doesn't drink. He no longer smokes. Typically he works and goes home. He reads books and spends time with his family. He doesn't seem to have any interest in friends, and certainly not any need of them. He doesn't seek people—not live ones, anyway. He is certainly not looking for acceptance. Part of him is always hidden. He is most definitely on the outside.

Each morning he slides into his persona and wears it like protective armor. It adds a little character and a lot of cheekiness. It enables him to become Mr. Crime Scene Cleaner. His weapons are not so much his scrapers and enzymes but his words, which surround him like a magnetic shield, working to prevent aspects of his work from getting in.

Neal fits the classic iconic hero because his actions are so very necessary. There is no getting around the fact that rooms tainted with blood must be cleaned. You couldn't, I imagine, sit in a living room watching television while ignoring a clump of the previous tenant's brain that has cemented itself to the ceiling. For families and friends who can't face these things, Neal is essential. He is a knight in a red T-shirt who saves the day.

I also think Neal has the classic internal struggle that true heroes have. They walk a thin line. They are heroic in their actions, but they could, it often seems, just as easily be on the wrong side of the line. They have the same traits as the bad guy, the same grit and determination, the same restlessness and need for conflict. Yet, they are not bad. Sometimes it seems like they end up on the good side simply to oppose something as strong-willed as themselves. It wasn't necessarily a choice; that was just the way the chips fell.

What happens to those with heroic tendencies when an outlet for heroism doesn't exist? Where would Neal be without Crime Scene Cleaners? I wonder. I just can't imagine him working in a bank for the rest of his days. Even though he said that this was once his line of thinking, I don't see him as a mortician, either, locked in a back room embalming stiffs, preparing the flowers and dusting the caskets, shaking hands with the bereaved.

Neal needs conflict. And death is the ultimate conflict. In all its forms, death is relentless and reliable.

This hero will never be without a villain to chase.

CRIME SCENE CLEANERS
PROMPT PROFESSIONAL TRAUMA SCENE CLEANING

Death, traumatic injury or hazardous contamination are events that few people ever plan to experience. Unfortunately, the problems that arise from these events are very difficult to deal with.

Crime Scene Cleaners Inc. is ready at all times to remedy any situation that may arise from such events. Our clients choose us for our proven expertise in providing prompt, professional cleanup services and restoring property to its original condition. Crime Scene Cleaners Inc. services all types of trauma, distressed property and biohazard scenes in communities across the United States. We are dedicated to assisting law enforcement, public service agencies and property owners/managers in restoring property that has been contaminated as a result of crime, disaster or misuse.

Crime Scene Cleaners Inc. is available to serve you 24 hours a day, 365 days a year. Please call our toll-free number for a prompt, free consultation. If you need more information on how a Crime Scene Cleaners Inc. team can be of service to you, call nationwide 1-800-357-XXXX

There aren't many people out there who, after watching a movie, think up a concept that will evolve into a company that today turns over more than 4 *million dollars* a year. But somehow, it doesn't surprise me that this is exactly what Neal Smither did.

The movie was *Pulp Fiction,* that great example of stylized violence that was one of the biggest hits of the nineties. If you've seen the movie, the scene that influenced Neal is easy to guess. It comes right after John Travolta's character, Vincent Vega, blows off Marvin's head in the back of the car, spraying blood and brain everywhere. It's the scene where Harvey Keitel's character, The Wolf, arrives to clean up the mess.

> THE WOLF: Good. What I need for you two fellas to do is take those products and clean the inside of the car. And I'm talkin' fast, fast, fast. You need to get in the backseat, scoop up all those little pieces of brain and skull. Get it out of there . . .

"I had been working in a bank, and was a fairly successful guy before I was made redundant," Neal tells me as we sit eating pancakes and drinking coffee in a diner. "I was there with my six months' redundancy money wondering what I wanted to do. Originally, I thought about being a mortician; ya know, I was looking for some stability." Neal starts to get animated as he pours syrup on his pancakes and reminisces; it's clear that he still gets a buzz from these memories of his. "Knowing that people are always gonna die, I thought, 'Hey, I could become a mortician, get a job, learn the ropes, and then start my own business.'"

There's a short pause while Neal stuffs half a pancake into his mouth, which he washes down with coffee. He seems to freeze for a second as he looks me in the eye with a big smile on his face, and then he continues.

"But then I saw *Pulp Fiction*. As I watched The Wolf, I was like, 'Hey, I could do that!' If I could stuff a body I sure as hell could do that, right? And once the idea was in my head, you know . . . I knew the police weren't cleaning up the murder scenes. I didn't see ma and pa on their hands and knees wiping Johnny's brains off the wall. So I did some research and thought, that's it—*'Crime Scene Cleaners.'*"

Neal applied for a business license at the same time as he took a job selling household appliances. He needed a regular job to keep him afloat while he started Crime Scene Cleaners. From there it was simply a case of setting his goal and picking the fastest, most direct route possible.

"There was so much that I needed to know. How much does the cleanup of a suicide cost? What are the health codes? What chemicals are used? What damage do the chemicals cause? Where do you dispose of the biohazards? So I bought myself a good answering machine—you know, the kind that took the large-format tapes—and I called existing cleaning companies and basically recorded the conversations so that I could review them for what I needed afterwards.

"I'm pretty aggressive. I called cleaning companies— janitorial, commercial, and residential. I got a job for about a week with Merry Maid, just to try and figure it all out. You know, I've always been a real clean guy but I'd never done it for a living. So I just wanted to work with them to see if there were any special tricks, but there weren't really any great tricks. I called other companies that were doing this and basically lied to them and got their information. I did what I had to do to get what I needed to get, pretty much. You know, 'How do you do it? How much is it gonna cost? Blah blah blah blah blah . . .' And I just kind of improved on what they were doing. You know, I'd be like, 'Hi, sorry to bother you, our daughter fell through our glass sliding door last night and we've got a good amount of blood and I just can't face cleaning it.' I'd give them a sob story, blah blah blah, then they'd give me the rundown and I'd say, 'Well, thank you very much, I'll call you back.' And I just kept calling all the companies out there, changing the scenario every time. I went from my imaginary daughter to my imaginary grandfather who'd died in his bed and hadn't been found for a month, that sort of stuff. First off I'd ask, how much? Then I'd ask, what would they use? Would it damage my wooden floor? I'd ask, do I have to dump the garbage myself? Of course I knew that I didn't, but by asking them they assured me that the garbage was taken to a biohazard landfill out at so-and-so. So then I was able to contact the landfill. And I always did it on a line that was blocked so they couldn't call *me* back. And it worked, you know. A lot of my early research and even my marketing practices, they're . . . they're *ethical* . . . but I don't know how many people would practice them. But I have no problem with them. I'm out to win."

At the beginning, not everybody shared Neal's winning attitude for Crime Scene Cleaners. Every bank he went to for investment turned him down. There was little encouragement to be had from friends or family, either.

"Crime Scene Cleaners! Are you nuts?" his best friend asked.

"That's never gonna work!" a cousin told him.

"*Oh my God,* that's just ridiculous. Who the hell are you going to sell to?" an uncle wanted to know.

Neal listened, but he wasn't deterred.

"It's so much easier to be negative than it is to be positive. I just was not interested in the negativity. I didn't need anybody's approval. I knew the concept of Crime Scene Cleaners was gonna work. So I just went straight ahead. I had my health code books written up. They cost a fortune, dude! And as soon as I had those and I was legal and all, I got straight on the phones. 'Hi, my name's Neal Smither, I'm the president of Crime Scene Cleaners.' They'd be like, '*Crime Scene Cleaners. What the hell is that?*' Then I would tell them what the hell we were: 'Well, we're a company specializing in the cleanup of murders, suicides, accidental death or extreme cleanups. I'd like to take a few minutes to introduce our company and our services and to let you know I'm not a wacko. . . .' "

Nine times out of ten, the people on the other end of the phone were so intrigued by the concept of Crime Scene Cleaners that they wanted to meet this strange man who was offering the strangest of services; no doubt so that they could confirm that he truly *was* a wacko and report him to the appropriate authorities. (As most of Neal's appointments were with police chiefs, the proper authorities were more often than not looking him straight in the eye.) But what they found when Neal Smither entered their offices was not a madman in a bloodstained pair of dungarees wielding an array of soiled utensils, but a man in a suit who was very serious about death and the removal of all visible traces of it.

Although Neal was rarely without a phone pressed to his ear, or not out visiting hundreds of people in a bid to get Crime Scene Cleaners embedded in their minds, he wasn't getting any actual jobs. Luckily, he was still working from the office of the appliance company, which his boss was fine with as long as he made his fifty-thousand-dollar monthly sales target. But his friends and family were starting to comment on the lack of work generated for Crime Scene Cleaners.

"Just face it, dude, your idea doesn't work!"

"Get out before you spend more money on this idea!"

"Your stubbornness is going to bankrupt you!"

Most people would have closed the books on Crime Scene Cleaners, taking the negative balance on the bank statement as a lesson learned. The printed stationery would have been thrown in the trash, the health-code books would have been stashed in the attic for the mice to eat, and the printed T-shirts would have been ripped up and used on Sundays for polishing the car.

"But I just kept telling myself, 'You are not wrong: *this works!*' And I kept going: more phone calls and more appointments. Even though it was costing me at that point more than I was making. I mean, I just went for it with American Express."

One day Neal's phone rang and on the other end of the line was a lady in distress. Her sister, who had been in her mid-fifties, had recently discovered that her cancer had come out of remission—*again*. There would be no more trips to the hospital, no more chemotherapy, no more watching her body die around her bones. Knowing that the doctors could do nothing, she took a gun and shot herself in the head, killing the cancer once and for all.

Neal was delighted.

"It actually wasn't that bad," he tells me with genuine surprise on his face. "Which, was good, 'cause I didn't really know what I was doing at that point. Meaning, I knew what to do, but I hadn't actually cleaned up a suicide before. But I could see there wasn't much of a problem. It was a good job to start with. The main thing, or the thing that I hadn't really thought about that much, was that I had to sit with the lady and help her to calm down. She was distraught, and I had to try and get her to relax so that I could explain exactly what it was I could do for her."

When the crying finally stopped, Neal calmly explained his services to the woman and told her how much it was going to cost.

"I hit her with a price and I knew immediately: '*Oh my God*, this is for me!' Because I'm good with people generally. I can speak real well when I need to. I was able to talk her down and get her to understand what it was I was pitching to her and I gave her the price and she didn't hesitate and I mean *not one bit*. She couldn't write the check fast enough. I had never seen anybody so keen to hand over money before. It was just *incredible*. I think, if I could have written the check out faster she would have had me do it. And I pretty much knew right there and then, 'Oh, Jesus Christ, *this* is for me.' Yeah! I was excited, dude; this is what I had been working towards. But still, I knew I had to do a good job—there's no excuse for a bad job in this game. It's very visual, you know. Clean means *clean*. You look and you look hard, that's how I did it on that first job, and I just kept doing it that way ever since. If two months down the line somebody finds a speck of blood under the handrail or some dried brain inside the lampshade, or a skull fragment in the potpourri, then you ain't getting recommended when her friend Doris's daughter slits her wrists on the living room floor, you know what I'm saying? And I want that job too. I want *all* the jobs."

Four weeks passed before Neal's phone rang again. It was a building supervisor from a residential complex in Oakland Hills.

"I didn't know shit about the job, but I could smell it from outside as soon as I got there, it was that bad. I could tell by the smell what it was going to be like. I called my sister and had her come out and help me."

An elderly man had died of natural causes on his sofa. The sofa was positioned in front of a large window that let in the hot Californian sun of mid-July. At first glance, the job wasn't as bad as Neal's nose had thought. The sofa had caught most of the body fluid. There was a small puddle underneath the sofa, but little more.

"Compared to the smell, the mess was relatively small and so it should've just been a case of pulling the couch and cleaning up the relatively small mess underneath. But the real funk—that didn't kick in until I jostled the couch, which stirred up all the liquids that had sat stationary for a month.

It was off the fucking chart, dude. So anyway, I grab the sofa just like, 'Oh, you're coming with me.' I picked up one end and body fluid just started to gush out the other end all over the wooden floor and, shit, *I just panicked.* I just could not believe my fucking eyes! *Or my nose!* The job started out as just your regular grandpa decomp, you know, but when it mixed it was just like a volcano of smells, man. To this day it's the worst thing I've ever smelled, by far. I'll never forget that one. The problem was it was so humid that this stuff never got the chance to dry up. It just putrefied and putrefied and putrefied! This stuff that was coming out—*let me tell ya*—was this thick brown grunge-type liquid. There was already more than a bucketful and I was panicking, 'cause I didn't know if I was gonna be able to clean this shit up, it was that bad. I was just freaking out. My sister was outside throwing up. I mean the guy had been like a four-hundred-pound dude, beached on the couch. The couch had caught everything and held it like a Ziploc. But I don't know, I guess adrenaline just took over, 'cause I just grabbed that motherfucker, and I was screaming, and I dragged it outta there. It was extremely heavy and hard to manhandle, but I just ripped that motherfucker out. Left a nice brown stripe behind me. But I just had to get it out—the leakage was going beyond anything I was capable of cleaning at the time."

Neal worked with the building supervisor again a few weeks later, but this time it was Neal who called him.

"I learned very quickly that the media are hungry for stories. If you look through the magazines and newspapers, there really aren't that many good stories to focus on. I knew by the reaction that I got from everybody who heard what I was doing that this was an intriguing subject. So I started contacting newspapers and magazines, radio stations, and soon everybody was just lining up to do a story on Crime Scene Cleaners. It was crazy. The building supervisor I told you about, from the whale decomp, he was doing interviews with me on the radio."

Today, Neal's office walls are lined with framed articles about Crime Scene Cleaners. Some he had shown me before, on my first visit. Many of them are new. As the years pass, the media outlets seem to get bigger. The articles on the wall start with the local presses, but over the last six years Crime Scene Cleaners has been covered by everybody from *Hustler* to the *San Francisco Tribune*. Even I had a call from CNN a year or so ago; they wanted me to do an interview about my time spent with Neal. The articles and the growing media attention, the increasing coverage of the outlets, seem to suggest that Neal is using the media for his own means after all, and rather successfully, too.

And they just keep coming.

"At least once a month I have a reporter or a film crew with me. Damn, I got this woman from Japan, she calls me up like twice a week to interview me at three fucking A.M. and she can't understand shit I say. She asks how much we make a year. I say, '*Midseven* figures.' And she's like, 'Wha mi se figa?' But I love it. Death sells. That's why, I mean, I knew when I started this that I was going with the name Crime Scene Cleaners. You've seen the way people look at my truck. That thing is so eye-catching. People can't believe what they're seeing. It really sticks in their minds, you know. They come up to me if I'm in a line in the bank or getting coffee, if I'm in one of my T-shirts, which I always am, and they'll be like, 'Crime Scene Cleaners! *Wow!* What's the worst thing you've ever seen?'"

It is ridiculous that it happens now, right as Neal is talking about being admired by his public, but five young guys have just entered the diner where Neal and I are sitting. They do not slide straight for a booth. They come down to us.

"Dude, is that your truck outside?"

I am sitting there thinking, *It has to be a setup, he* must *be paying them.*

Neal looks at me and gestures to the boys. "You see. *Freaks,* man."

And as Neal and I sit there laughing, one of them adds, *"Awesome!"*

They crowd around the booth and without missing a beat start asking about jobs. Actually, one specific job. It seems one of the kids saw Neal's trucks parked outside a house on his own street. He wants some details. But Neal isn't biting.

Something catches Neal's eye out the window. Parked in front of his truck is a very shiny, very fast-looking sports car.

"Is that yours?" he asks the kid who is doing most of the talking.

The kid smiles; he could not be any happier right now.

"Yeah," he says.

"That's a fucking fast car, dude!" Neal says very seriously.

"It's off the chart," the kid agrees. "I've had that—"

"Dude," Neal cuts him off. "Be careful. Or you're gonna have me scraping your brains off the road one day."

All the boys erupt into laughter.

The waitress comes over and hands them several bags

packed with food. It seems they were waiting for take-out. A few seconds pass before they spin away from the curb.

Turning to me, Neal says, "Where was I?" He signals to the waitress for more coffee and continues from where we had left off. "Oh yeah, but I *never* turn down press. I want this company to be the best, the biggest, and the most successful. I'm a pretty impatient guy. I'm very type A and extremely competitive, and all of that on top of itself tends to make for a fairly formidable—you know—opponent. 'Cause I'll tell ya, I won't be as smart as everyone but I'll fucking outwork ya. I just *will* outwork ya and I'll play a lot dirtier, too. You know, you better wanna win with me because I *do* want to win and I make no bones about it. The difference between us and other companies that do this is they try to get rich off every single job! We don't, 'cause I want *all* the jobs, and we'll do them at a decent price—and we get them. One of our biggest competitors back east, he does the cleanup but they make most of their money on the restoration, so they don't have to do a good cleanup job 'cause they're gonna rip the shit out of the place and rebuild it and double bang 'em and make more money on the rebuild. Which is clever, but I don't have that skill. I'm a janitor, I can clean anything, but I can't drive a nail to save my life.

"What you gotta know is, when I started I didn't get a job for months. At the start it was just me and my Chevy Geo Metro, my briefcase, and my phone. And I was an anal nervous wreck: 'Oh my God, I've spent all this money and nothing's happening, why isn't it going?' But I just kept bombarding people, got my name out there. I knew that once people knew about me and what I was doing, this shit would advertise itself. Gore sells, my friend! Initially my goal was one job a month, then it went to one job a week and then three jobs a week, then one a day, and then it was, 'I wanna make a thousand bucks a day,' and so on and so forth. Now in the Bay Area alone we're doing around a hundred fifty jobs a month. You gotta realize . . . I mean just look around, this country is shit scared of death, you know what I'm saying? So if you can be the middleman between them and death, they'll pay you a shitload of dough!"

The next job is a callback and Neal is not happy about it. Politely, he explains why to the customer.

"Doctor, the real-estate agent called in two companies to bid on this job originally—myself and my biggest competitor in the area. She bid ten thousand dollars for the job, which of course I didn't know. I bid forty-six hundred. So of course I get the job. Now, when that job is done, the real-estate agent goes and hires my biggest competitor, who originally bid the ten thousand, and he gets her in to inspect *my* work. So do you think she's gonna find something? She has to. She's gotta try and justify what her other five grand was for because the real-estate agent ain't gonna call her again if he finds out she costs twice the going rate."

"I understand that," the doctor says. "But I gotta problem: the house is sold and the buyer won't complete until this is—"

"*Sir,* don't you worry. It's gonna be dealt with today, I assure you. But, *you know,* I'll clean up in the attic again, but I think you need to get your exterminator back, and if after today you find rat droppings up there again . . . *you know what I'm saying?* If your exterminator guy hasn't dealt with the problem on his side, then you're gonna be calling us every day."

As Neal works up in the musky, dark attic, collecting rat droppings and spraying the floor with enzyme, I ask him if he often bumps heads with this competitor.

"Oh, now and again, you know."

"Do you know her personally?"

"Oh yeah, she used to work for me."

"She did?" I ask, surprised.

"Yeah, she was with me for some months, and once she thought she knew it all she went off and started her own company."

"Does it bother you that she did that?"

"Bother me? *Hell no*. Hey, it's what I did. What's good for me is good for everybody else. What bothers me is this kind of bullshit, where she tries to muddy my name. She should never be inspecting my work. Any idiot knows you don't have neighboring competitors inspect each other's work. She was probably embarrassed at having bid five grand more than me for the same job. I would have been. She probably took one look at the house, was introduced to the doc, and just saw dollar signs, you know. But that's fine, she can play any way she wants, it doesn't bother me none. When I start to hear that she does a better cleanup than me, then I'll pay attention. Until then, I don't really pay her much mind. But this is bullshit; I never try to get work by putting other companies down or picking fault in what they do."

As unbelievable as that may sound, I can vouch for Neal's word on this. I overheard him on the phone this morning with a customer who was making an inquiry. When Neal gave an estimate for the job, the customer must have thought it high. I listened as Neal recommended two other companies, told the customer that they both have good reputations, and that the wise thing to do would be to have all three companies come and quote on the job.

Crime Scene Cleaners currently bills over $4 million a year. The success of the company is down largely to Neal's marketing strategy, which focuses on death, the peculiarity of his company, and the bizarreness of his own character. He is anal about doing the best cleanup, but he grabs media attention by playing to the continual need for entertainment. It's what enabled him to stride ahead of his conservative competition early on. Before Neal launched Crime Scene Cleaners, companies with regular-sounding cleaning-company names used to be the only people to call for crime scene cleanup. Sure, they were certified to clean up biohazards, but none of them marketed death as Neal did; they marketed only cleaning.

"A cleaning company is a cleaning company is a cleaning company. 'I got a shitload of blood to clean, should I call PPF Cleaners? Sullivan and Sullivan Janitorial Services? Miraculous Maids or Crime Scene . . . What the fuuuuck . . . ? Specializing in homicide, suicide . . .' That's normally when my phone rings. People generally don't forget the name of my company."

Neal is right—people generally don't forget him or the name of his company, and that fact has not gone unnoticed. Over the last few years, several other companies have cropped up, offering the same service under a similar name and actually trying their damnedest to be Neal Smither. I have had phone calls from them, after they saw my original article on

Neal, asking me to go out and write about them. I wasn't interested because I already had the Crime Scene Cleaner story, but during these conversations and e-mails I couldn't help but notice an undertone of jealousy. One guy seemed positively angry that I wouldn't write about him. It apparently wasn't fair that I would write about Neal and not him. Where was the justice?

What I noticed through these little chinwags and correspondences was that the people who were following in Neal's footsteps seemed to be doing it largely for the fame. They were after notoriety. They wanted press about *themselves*. Neal wants press about Crime Scene Cleaners, and he will do most of it, but he would just as happily, and often does, let journalists follow one of his other workers. Neal is not driven by fame or having his picture in the paper; he is driven by removing all traces of the recently dead, and money. That's why he is more marketable than those who have followed in his footsteps. He came up with the idea of Crime Scene Cleaners and fought for it, was anal about its success. The cleaners I spoke to got their idea after seeing footage of Neal. It's as if after seeing him they seemed to think, *Hey, that's a cool idea. If I clean dead people I'll end up on TV. I'll be a celebrity in the local bar.*

But Neal doesn't have that desire. Neal is an especially unusual individual and I saw this from the moment I met him, on pretty much an hourly basis. It wasn't just the shock tactics. He had many and varied ways of surprising me.

One midafternoon we were on the road, speeding from job to job and checking up on the staff. The phone wouldn't stop ringing and Neal was doing his no-handed kamikaze driving routine. There were three police cars that needed to be cleaned of blood and vomit. We rushed over to make sure that the job was being handled properly by the staff. Neal at that point wasn't getting his hands dirty; his art at that moment was one of delegation.

"Man, I'm feeling burnt out now right now, I just can't clean right now. Luckily, I have a lot of staff."

"Why are you burnt out? Did something happen?" I asked.

"Yeah, you could say that. I was on a cleanup, a suicide decomp. The body had been lying on the kitchen floor for a *long, long fucking time*. There was shit everywhere; you know, after a time the body just oozes liquid, the whole thing just liquefies; the maggots get it. I slipped in some shit and I went down right in the middle of it. Oooh yeah, that was groovy! I was slipping around in shit, blood, spinal fluid, maggots; the works. I mean, I couldn't get up. I was just slipping and sliding in this goo, in this human fluid. Oh, it freaked me out just a little bit . . . *ooooooooooooooh*." Neal gave an uncharacteristic shudder before answering his cell phone. "Okay, what's the address? Has Eric finished the last job? Ok, send him over and tell him to suit up. I'll be there soon to price up."

After checking on his staff and the police cars, we got back into Neal's truck and drove in silence for a couple of minutes. To break the quiet I asked Neal what the job was that we were heading to.

"Suicide," he said matter-of-factly. "Alan, I wake up every morning and pray for death and it just keeps coming."

The house we arrived at was completely smashed. Furniture was upside down. Drawers were splintered across the floor, and their contents spread everywhere. Every room seemed to be in the same condition. The smell was rank, but tolerable in comparison with a decomp earlier that day. Standing in the main bedroom was the wife of the suicide, attended to by Neal, Eric (a young, shaved-headed twentysomething who had been working for Neal three months), and myself.

We all stood in silence, looking at the splattered wall.

"High-caliber pistol to the head?" Neal asked eventually.

"Yeah," the wife answered, sounding slightly impressed by Neal's observation.

"The brain matter on the wall gives it away," Neal replied. "Anyway, here's what we'll do. Everything with matter on it will be pulled and burned. The bed, the sheets, comforter, pillows, and carpet will all go into the furnace. We'll pull the baseboards from the bottom of the wall in that corner where all the blood is concentrated. Once the carpet's gone, we'll scrub the boards where the blood is, get out what we can, then we paint a sealant over it so nothing can get out and nothing can rot. We'll deodorize the whole house 'cause it smells pretty funky in here. We dispose of everything, it's all burned, and you don't have to worry about a thing."

"How much is this all going to cost?" the wife asked.

"Eleven hundred bucks," Neal stated.

"Will it still smell?"

"No, ma'am, you won't even know what's happened in this room after we're finished with it . . . except for the fact that . . . well, you know." Neal seemed to freeze for a second. I was wondering what had happened—had he said the wrong number? Had he meant twenty-one hundred and just realized his error? "Hey," he said with some urgency. "Is that an original Nagel on the wall?" asked Neal, drawing everybody's attention to an 1980s art-deco-style painting of a woman with her hair tied up as she looks back over her shoulder, out of the canvas.

"Yeah," the wife replied. "Do you know the artist?"

"Sure. That's gotta be worth some bucks right there, an original signed Nagel, especially now that he's dead."

"Well, we paid twenty-five hundred for it about ten years ago."

"It's gotta be worth three or four times that now . . . you know, what with him being dead."

As Neal said this I couldn't help but wonder how he knew of this artist; he didn't strike me as an art lover. How did he know Nagel was dead? Maybe he cleaned up the artist . . . you know, *what with him being dead.*

I asked him when we were alone if that was the case. "Dude," he replied. "I like art!"

MAN IN THE BATH PART I:
THE VIRGIN AND THE FLY

Neal discovered my disgust for the maggot on the job where he spotted the Patrick Nagel painting. The deceased had been on the outer circle of the Hells Angels. He had taken himself on a major meth binge and blown his brains out all over the walls. It was a hot day, and stupidly, I admit now, I was wearing shorts and sandals. I remember looking at the bed as a maggot fell to the floor. I looked at the floor and discovered it was covered in maggots. I followed their pattern and discovered that they were everywhere. They were scattered around my sandaled feet.

I started to run.

As I dashed across the room I could see the maggots flicking up around me; I could feel them as they bounced off my calves and landed on top of my feet.

A couple caught in my leg hair.

I tried to brush them off as I ran down the stairs. At this

point I knew vomit to be inevitable. I tripped and fumbled my way to the front door and managed to drag myself outside quickly enough to throw up in a plant pot.

Neal, as well you can imagine, was duly entertained. He gave me a plastic bag to collect my vomit in.

Last summer, while I was talking to publishers about this book, I called Neal. It was midmorning in San Francisco. He answered the phone with his usual aplomb.

"Neal!"

"Hey, Neal, it's Alan."

"Oh, Alan dude, you've got to see what I have in front of me right now!" Neal's volume jumped several decibels. "This guy has been murdered by his gay lover, who left him in the bathtub, where he decomped for a month. This is some funky, off-the-chart shit. And I know you love maggots. Here, listen to this—you can hear them. Can you hear that?"

The line went silent for a few seconds while Neal held the phone over the bathtub so that I could enjoy the maggots. He was right, I could hear them, crawling around in a frenzy, sucking, nibbling, and generally getting their fill of what used to be Gary Lee Ober. They made a sound of hamburger meat being kneaded and mashed.

"The smell is just *off the fucking chart*!" Neal said, jumping back on the line. "You can smell it down the street!"

Although the body appears free of decay immediately after death, there are bacteria inside that feed off the contents of the intestines. When the body dies, the bacteria start eating the intestine itself. Eventually, they eat their way out of the intestine and start eating the surrounding organs. Certain flies (if you are interested in who these chaps are, I refer you to the blowfly, the bottle fly, and the common house fly) can pick up the scent of death as if they knew beforehand that a life was about to be extinguished. They are not fussy: natural causes, suicide, murder—it means nothing to the fly. They arrive on the scene within minutes to deposit their eggs in the still-tender flesh that will nurture the eggs until they hatch. They go for openings—nostrils, ears, eyes, or wounds. Once the flies have housed their eggs, it would normally take about eight to fifteen hours for the eggs to hatch (although this varies according to temperature). It takes a similar amount of time for the first larvae to develop. They feed on liquid protein. Once fully developed, they spend a few days dining on the delicacies of the flesh, using their sharp-hooked mouths to tear at it. Another week and the maggots complete their growth and leave the body to become pupae, soon themselves to become airborne, dive-bombing flies planting their own eggs to start the next generation. The cycle from egg to maggot to fly takes from two to three weeks.

A pack of maggots can devour human tissue at startling speed. When they swarm, they dive into the flesh and rip away at it, then wiggle to the top of the swarm for air before they dive back again for another mouthful. It's a frenzied pack, maggots going up and maggots going down. The heat produced by the all-consuming pack is enough to maintain larvae growth at low temperatures.

The bacteria are also at work breaking down tissues and cells. Fluids are released into body cavities and various gases are produced: hydrogen sulfide, methane, cadaverine, and putrescine. The gases intensify the growth of the bacteria, which in turn creates a pressure buildup. This pressure inflates the body and forces fluids out of cells and blood vessels and into the body cavity.

The decay process gathers speed as it goes. The fluids and gases that leak from the body attract even more blowflies, flesh flies, beetles, and mites. Some of the latecomers are themselves predatory, and eat the maggots as well as the rotting flesh.

By week two, the body will probably collapse. Exposed body parts and flesh are blackened, and the smell is intense. Large amounts of body fluids seep out, attracting other insects to feed. At this point, there are generally several generations of insects feeding on the body.

"Alan, this is Shawn," says Neal, introducing one of his employees. We are at the scene of a shotgun suicide that has for the most part been cleaned up. Shawn has just finished emptying the place out to get it ready for renting again.

"You remember when I spoke to you last year, the dead gay guy? The maggots?" Neal continues. "It was Shawn that did the cleanup. You guys should hang out; Shawn will have some good stories for you."

"That would be great if you have time one day," I say to Shawn. "When would be good for you?"

"Well, I'm done for the day," Shawn says. "So, you wanna go grab a beer?"

In my rental car, I follow Shawn's white Crime Scene Cleaners truck as we drive to a bar on his route home. We install ourselves on bar stools, order drinks, and quickly get down to it.

"I was still pretty much a virgin," begins Shawn.

I can tell straightaway, from the way Shawn delivers this line, from his tone, that he is no stranger to telling stories. He has a wonderful energy. There's a bright light burning inside Shawn. I know already that I am going to like him.

The bar we are sitting in is called The Ivy Room. It's dark and murky, with a long black bar. Most of the people at the bar are drinking shots. The music is loud; the conversation, when it sporadically exists, is louder. It's exactly the kind of place where you would expect to have found Charles Bukowski, quietly necking whiskeys before punching a loudmouth in the face. It's five in the afternoon and the handful of bar patrons are drunk. This is a place where the men wear vests and baseball caps or have slicked-back hair. The women seem to make a bit more effort, but are clearly overdone. So overdone, in fact, that I am wondering what they charge. The two women sitting next to us at the bar are plastered, both physically and metaphorically.

Shawn is wearing jeans and his white Crime Scene Cleaners, Inc. T-shirt. His company baseball cap sits on the bar. It's an odd place to bring me, this rundown little whiskey joint, but it sure beats shiny and new Walnut Creek, the town where I am staying while working on this story. Maybe Shawn knew that I needed to get away from the Gap kids, that I was in desperate need of something more working-class, closer to my own roots.

Shawn is a very interesting character. From the outside, you could expect anybody working as a crime scene cleaner to be, as Shawn so delicately put it, a "knucklehead." But Shawn is no knucklehead. He is a smart guy. He studied art history and has had his own work shown at the San Diego Modern Art Museum. He's not what you might call typical for the job, but then those who want the job purely for the blood generally burn out after a few months. Shawn is the company's longest-lasting employee, having been with Neal for eighteen months. One and a half years of death have not dampened his warm smile and excellent manners. You get what you see with Shawn, a well-mannered, handsome, if a little baby-faced, guy. I imagine that his girlfriend is spoiled with chivalry.

"I think the guy in the bath was actually my first de-comp," he continues. "You know, Neal was there with me, I guess at the start. For my first three months Neal was at every job I did. He was there *before* me every time. On this job, I guess he knew what I was about and he was just like, *here's what you gotta do, here's what you gotta do, here's what you gotta do,* and he just left."

"Really? It was that bad and he left it to you?"

Shawn laughs. "Basically, yeah. He did all the shuck-and-jive bullshitting with the client and then just left me there. The entire apartment was just packed, I mean literally just packed full of stuff, and disheveled, too. I opened up the bathroom and the bathroom was *black*. There were so many flies and maggots, and when the maggots hatch they come out of these little tiny cocoon-type deals and they get dry and crusty. Basically, they're like Rice Krispies, but they're black! And then the flies eat everything, and flies regurgitate this *enzyme* to break down what they eat and then they suck it back up, so they're just sitting there doing this just all over every surface in this bathroom from floor to ceiling. So I open it up, and, literally, everything is stained. It was a typical bathroom, white walls, white toilet, white sink, and everything's just covered in these brown and black specks. The bathroom floor was covered in an inch of dead flies and the husks left by the maggots when they hatch. There's still, like tons of live flies floating around, and they're so heavy, so fat and bloated from eating on this guy. I mean they weren't even like flying. They were just hopping around. They were getting ready to lay their next round. I could not believe what I was seeing. I was just blown away, literally blown away."

"How did all the stuff get all over the walls?" I ask.

"Oh, that's the flies. It's just them landing and stuff. I mean this guy had been there for so long there was a puddle in the tub. The tub was half full with body fluids, and the kicker of it was, this is just my assumption, the guy—jilted lover or what have you—I think after he had committed the murder he was just in there taking a dump on the body. I mean, I don't know why. There was so much actual human waste in the tub, it didn't seem feasible that it could have gotten in there any other way. The fluid in the tub was just goo, thick black goo, with a consistency like thick honey. It was actually my first experience of dealing with feces in any volume. You wipe your ass every day, but you have tissue, so . . . This stuff is just like glue, like this oily, nasty *errrrrrrrrgh!* And the . . . the smell? If you smell fresh blood in any kind of quantity . . . the only way I can describe it . . . you know, have you ever licked a nine-volt battery? Forget the shock, but the taste of the battery. That's fresh blood. But *this* smell was like every nasty funk you can possibly imagine, all wrapped into one."

Shawn's face is starting to screw up a little. Jim McKinnon, the man charged with Gary Lee Ober's murder, had lived in the apartment while Ober decomposed in the bathroom.

You can tell that Shawn struggles to understand how he lived with it.

"Did it make you sick, the bathroom?"

"I've only gotten close to throwing up on one job. It was a fridge that we were stripping from a house and it had rotten meat in it. It cracked open when we moved it and little bit of juice hit the floor, and it was just funk and I had to get out. So the only time I have come close to being sick on a job it was because of rotten meat in the fridge, not the mess I was there to clean. But no, I've never lost it. This was my first major job and I wanted to keep it together. I told myself I was gonna do a bang-up job. I put my respirator on, I double gloved, I put my Tyvek on, and I literally just started cleaning my way in. You know, I just kept chipping away and scrubbing with my brushes. I mean it took me eight hours of doing this over and over and over again. Eight hours of spray-wipe-scrub, spray-wipe-scrub, spray-wipe-scrub until I got to the bathtub, and then I was excited. I was like, 'I'm finally at the bathtub.' You gotta realize it was only like four feet away, you know. I mean I was focusing on the floor, the walls, the door, the ceiling, the toilet. I was standing on the toilet to reach the ceiling. The ceiling actually wasn't that bad. I guess it's hard for the flies to hang upside down there when they're, like, all gorged on this dude."

"How much mess can these flies really make?" I ask, somewhat doubtfully.

"A lot! I mean it was like . . . a lot! You have to remember they had been there for weeks."

"But I understand that they land on the guy, in all the gore, they get this stuff on themselves and then fly off and land somewhere else, but can they really cover the walls? *Were the walls really covered?*"

"*With their shit*—dude, flies shit, too!" Shawn's tone, expression, and the way he fidgets in his seat tell me that he means business. "You know, so they flew, took a shit, landed in the decomp, flew, spread that junk around, went back, ate some more, flew, took another shit. We're talking about thousands upon thousands of flies here."

Shawn and I refresh our drinks. While the barman is pouring, I sit back and try to take on board the scene Shawn is describing. It's not easy to do. I can't even begin to imagine how I would cope with cleaning such a scene.

"So I finally make it to the tub and I just reach my hands in. I made sure my gloves were pulled all the way up so that nothing went inside. You know, I'm trying to think of the logical way to do it. Nobody's in there holding my hand, I'm totally alone, *freaking out!* I reached in there and at the bottom, below the liquid, it was like hitting clay. And so I'm like, whatever this is, I'm gonna just scoop it up and put it in my bag, and of course I have both hands in there and I go to scoop it out and I go to put it in the bag and it won't even let go. I mean it was like . . . it was just stuck to my hands and I was like, *fuuuuuck!* What the fuck? This is bullshit! 'Cause I was double gloved, I just eased out of the gloves over the bag and put on another two pairs. Then I thought, *Well, I'm gonna wait on doing this bottom part. I'm gonna clean everything else and do the tub last.* So I grabbed the shower and used it to spray stuff down. And so I was scrubbing and doing the enzyme and spraying and I thought, *Wow, this is great,* and I started spraying other stuff, you know, the walls and fittings, and I was just letting it go on the floor and I was gonna wipe all that up. And the tub's filling, and the tub's filling and it's getting to the point where, you know, it's getting close to the top. And I'm just about done cleaning most of the walls at this point and it dawns on me, I'm like, I don't even know if this tub works. So I start hitting the little lever and it's *plugged! The tub!* The guy's been in it for so long that his goo plugged up the bathtub. And I'm like, oh, great, so now I have a bathtub full of this just awful . . . And I'm freaking out. I'm like, the last thing I have to do is clean out this tub and work my way out and I'm fucked. I need a plumber. I got myself so stressed out that I had to call Neal and said, 'Look, Neal, I thought I was doing the right thing but it looks like I've really fucked up,' and he was like, 'Well, does he have any towels? Any sheets, any blankets?' And I'm like, 'Yeah, there's a whole house full of shit.' He was like, 'Well, grab every blanket, towel, pillow—whatever you can get your hands on, and soak it all up.' And that's exactly what I did. I just soaked it up, just sponged it up. And it was great because it was all the dead guy's stuff, so I could just take all these towels and just soak that shit up. I was soaking, scooping, and wrapping— and the towels ended up like these oversized raviolis, you know. They were nasty. The soaking up took about two hours. Then I went down and got a putty knife, and I was just scraping and scooping the claylike goo with the putty knife, until I got to the point where it was doable and I could do what I'm used to doing and that's spraying the enzyme and cleaning. Then I took a gallon bottle of bleach, pumped it up in the pressure spray and just pushed it down that drain and just blasted the hell out of it. But still, I told them they needed a plumber. *Then* (and this really pissed me off) I picked the bag out of the bin in the kitchen. I was just thinking I should take the garbage out—that's gonna rot and go nasty, I can just take it with me. So I lift the bag out, I look back in the empty bin, and it was just full of maggots and I was like, why are there so many maggots there? I opened up the bag and it was just full of shit! I couldn't fucking believe it. I said it out loud: 'This is a big bag of shit!' "

A week or so later, Shawn was called back to the apartment to empty it of all its remaining possessions. He began to find things out about the fluids that he had previously removed, little details that stopped Gary Lee from being a blocked bathtub and reminded Shawn that he was a human being.

"It's so sad, you know, when you learn a little something about the people who you're cleaning. And this guy, whoever he was, was into classical music and wood carving. He was a coin collector, a Vietnam veteran. It wasn't bad enough that this other guy killed him; one of the downstairs neighbors told me that this guy had been selling all his stuff to fund his partying and even had them over for drinks one night while the dead guy was rotting in the tub. Like at the very beginning. He had told them the toilet was out of order so they wouldn't go in the bathroom."

The sadness doesn't end once the decomposed body has been cleaned up.

"While I was emptying the apartment, this guy knocked on the door and he was like, 'Can I get the VCR?' "

"What did you say?"

"Well, I didn't say yes. I just put the stuff on the back of the truck and people just took what they wanted; they were like, 'Well, he doesn't need it.'"

"What? Were they not concerned about catching something? I want to disinfect myself whenever you guys drive past me. I mean, what are they thinking? That's fucked?"

"Dude, that's not fucked. That's life."

At this point a drunk, but very attractive, black girl approaches Shawn.

"Hey, can I ask you a question?" She smiles.

"Sure," Shawn replies with a big grin.

"Could you get me a job with Crime Scene Cleaners?"

Shawn and I both laugh.

"No, I'm serious," she says. "I see the trucks around all the time and I keep meaning to call you guys for a job."

"What are you doing for a job now?" Shawn asks.

"I'm an actress. But still, I would like to do some Crime Scene Cleaning."

Shawn gives her a business card. We watch her as she shimmies out of the bar for a cigarette.

"She's never getting a job with Neal, I can tell you that." Shawn laughs. "Mind you," he adds, "I'd be more shocked if she even called him up."

"Do lots of people ask you if they can get a job?" I ask.

"Yeah, they do, actually. But you rarely actually hear back from them."

HEPATITIS C YOU LATER

As I approach the door, I see a small bouquet of yellow flowers poking out from a dirty brown glass. There are two other glasses: one holding clear water and another holding a burned-down, extinguished candle. Thrown on the floor next to the door are several feet of the bright yellow crime scene tape, with a plastic-wrapped telephone directory poking out from underneath. It looks terribly lonely, this little shrine.

The closed door looms, appearing bigger than it actually is, appearing to have some kind of energy, as if standing sentinel over a terrible secret. I can't help but think we shouldn't open it. Maybe when people die in a room, in an apartment, it should just be sealed off and left. I wish the door had already been open when we arrived.

Inside is an even sadder scene. Even though I caught the smell from outside, with the door closed, I wasn't prepared for the smell on the inside.

"Does it smell?" asks Jake as he watches my reaction.

Jake, the Crime Scene Cleaners' technician for this job, has been with the company for about six months. He is already wearing a blue protective suit with the top half pulled down and tied around his waist. He's about five feet ten, with a blond army-regulation haircut, short around the back and sides and brushed up on top.

"I don't really smell it much anymore," he says, pulling on a pair of rubber gloves.

But I can't answer. The only words I can muster are swimming around in my mind.

Don't be sick!

Don't be sick!

Don't be sick!

My hand is covering my mouth and nose, but to little effect. I know I have to continue, to enter the room properly. This is what I came here to document, after all. But the farther in I go, the worse the smell gets, the *thicker* it gets. It's really hard to describe this smell, because to give you a full breakdown I would have to open up my lungs and welcome the odor in.

The apartment is small, with a shared kitchen and living room and lots of black ash furniture. At the opposite end to the front door there is a countertop protruding from the wall on the right-hand side. This serves as a partition between living room and kitchen. The living-room sofa is also along the right-hand wall, with a big-screen TV system opposite. Large stacks of DVDs are piled up all around. There are the obvious guy choices: *The Usual Suspects*; *Fight Club*; *Seven*; *Full Metal Jacket*; and so on.

As I pass the counter, I notice the flies circling. I also notice the bloodstained kitchen linoleum.

Think shock.

Think gag.

"Can you see the body outline?" asks Jake.

No, I can't. I see only a smeared, burgundy mess, and I tell him so.

"Well, you got a leg right here," Jake says, pointing at a blood smear. "A leg there. That is the body right there. That's the head. That's the left arm, *probably,* and that's the right arm coming down. More than likely, if you can see by the way his head's turned, if you were to lie like this with your arm up . . ." Jake is leaning back over the linoleum, waving his arms about as he tries to maintain balance. It looks like any second now, and just to make sure I am crystal clear on the positioning, he's actually going to lie down in the blood and shape himself to fit the bloodstain. "You usually don't lie like this, right?" he continues. "So he was lying like this. Does that make sense?"

I have to admit that it is starting to take shape. Now that I have control over my bodily functions, and thanks to Jake's wonderful assistance, of course, I can in fact see the outline of a body. It's so clear now that I don't know how I managed to miss it to begin with.

"And then this is the top of the head, or the mouth, or whatever, where it's all dribbled out."

Without any doubt, Jake is really enjoying having somebody to talk to. And when I consider the average day of a crime scene cleaner, it must be a lonely job. You get the odd command shouted down the phone by Neal, the businesslike handshake of a relative, a brief chat with a motel manager, but then you are left alone. It must be a little creepy, too. Not only to find yourself alone in a room where somebody just died, but to be actually scraping them off the walls or floor. I totally understand why Jake has a continual flurry of words leaving his mouth. The energy in a room where somebody recently died has to be less eerie when there are two of you, when there's chatter.

"Looks like most of the trauma is coming from right here, the very top of the head."

Jake has to be a big fan of crime drama. I mean a *big* fan. I am thinking DVD collections, entire seasons watched and re-watched. Just like some of the dramatized crime-busting TV heroes, Jake has a theory, and like those good-looking stylized idols, he is going to pursue it to the very end. Even in the face of doubt, there is simply no stopping the guy.

"My guess would be that, you got a Zig-Zag roller up here on the counter; you see the evidence of marijuana right there? He was probably a dealer. It's right here in this area, which probably means that you're standing here to do your deal, right?" Jake stands with his back to the blood, demonstrating how the deceased might have stood in the midst of a narcotics transaction. "You know, here's the Zig-Zag roller, so he's probably selling dope. . . ."

I have to suppress a laugh here. It seems a bit of a leap to assume that ownership of a Zig-Zag roller makes you a drug dealer. In fact, for me, it suggests the exact opposite. I've seen an Italian girl roll a joint one-handed (she had broken her arm when riding her scooter while smoking). I've met marijuana dealers who can roll a joint with willpower alone. In fact, if anything, the Zig-Zag roller better represents somebody who does not deal drugs, who in fact rarely even partakes in drugs. But there's still no stopping Jake. He is having so much fun, and I don't see any reason to spoil it by interrupting him with my opinions.

". . . Someone came up from behind him here, like this." Jake now has one of his arms raised, doing an impression of the shadow that fell across the shower curtain in the film *Psycho,* as he plunges his arm down. "Then he fell forward, tried to put his hand out to stop, and just fell down."

There's a pause as we both stand staring at the bloodstain

"I mean, that's my guess," Jake says a little awkwardly.

Case solved, I think to myself.

This actually seems, even to me, like an easy job. It's a small floor, maximum twenty square feet. You can see where the blood reached the edge of the linoleum and seeped underneath, which means that the linoleum has to come up. In fact, there isn't really any cleaning to be done, just some physical shifting of the oven and the refrigerator and then the removing of the linoleum.

"This is pretty easy, right, Jake?"

"This? Yeah. I mean, even if I wasn't pulling up the flooring this would be easy. The nice thing about working with blood is that as soon as it hits oxygen it starts to coagulate. Once it's coagulated, it's really easy to clean off surfaces like this."

The smell is really starting to bother me now. It's worse when I open my mouth and try to talk. I dry retch a couple of times and head outside for some air.

The apartment is in the middle of a complex in a town called Mountain View. We are about thirty-five miles out of

San Francisco, in the heart of the Silicon Valley. With its neatly cropped lawns and family housing, it's a fairly typical Californian suburb. The demographics show that the neighborhood is 51 percent white, 22 percent Asian, 20 percent Hispanic, 3 percent black, and 4 percent other. The lifestyle here at the complex isn't on the lowest rung of the poverty ladder, but it would take only a small slip to get there. The people coming and going from the apartments or working on the grounds are mostly Hispanic.

"Hi. Do you know what happened to the guy in there?" I ask a man as he unlocks his car. He is short, wearing jeans and a gray T-shirt. He furrows his mustache as he looks me over.

"Who are you?" he quite rightly asks, suspicious, possibly, of sensationalist journalism.

"I'm with Crime Scene Cleaners," I tell him, half truthfully.

"Oh, you cleaning it up?"

"Yeah."

"Is it bad? Is there a lot of blood?"

"A fair bit," I tell him. "What happened here, do you know?"

"He was shot in the head, *twice*."

The cold reality of this information staggers me, and I realize it is wrong of me to be asking these questions.

"He seemed like a nice guy, too," the man continues. "I always see him out here working on his car and shit." He points to an old white Honda hatchback parked in the lot.

"You heard the shots?" I ask

"My wife heard them. Does it smell?" he asks, a little urgently.

"It's pretty bad," I tell him, doing a good job of organizing my expression accordingly.

"Oh, it must be bad if you think it's bad. You must see a lot of this shit, right? So, does it just smell—or does it, like, *really* smell?"

Fear and murder have no bearing on my reality. I live in Copenhagen, where for the most part we ride our bicycles from café to café and drink overpriced lattes. I am never (except when riding said bicycle home while drunk) in fear for my safety. But then Denmark is a small country, and I live in a capital city that has a small-town community vibe. I do not live in a city where people are shot and murdered on a regular basis. If somebody gets murdered in Copenhagen, regardless of what else might be going on in the media, it's a big story. This is a country where murder, even the dullest, most uninventive kind, is still newsworthy. But, of course, that's not true of the big cities of the United States. In many U.S. cities people live with such fears and concerns continually. There are neighborhoods where people die unnatural deaths on a weekly basis. There are people out there who don't expect to see their thirtieth birthdays and who quite probably won't. This neighborhood doesn't look that bad, but it's bad enough that a guy who lived in the apartment Jake is cleaning was shot twice in the head. There's enough to be concerned about there alone. But the man before me here is not concerned with the double whammy to the head, his only concern is having me rank the strength of the odor.

"But, like, on a scale of one to ten, this is what?"

As I walk back to the building, another neighbor stops me.

"Will you be done in there today?" asks the lady holding

her little daughter's hand. She is wearing a fluorescent orange T-shirt tucked into her jeans. Her daughter wears black leggings, a pink and white stripy vest, and jelly sandals.

"Yes, another hour at the most." I smile. "Do you know what happened?" I jump a little as I ask this question. Mostly because I don't know why I have asked it. I already have the answer, but the question just pops out before I can stop it. I feel bad for asking about something so horrid in front of her daughter. It was stupid. I wasn't thinking. "*I'm sorry. I . . .*"

"He was stabbed in the chest a bunch a times," the woman tells me matter-of-factly. "My friend is a friend of his mother's. It was drug related."

Hmm. That bloody Zig-Zag again.

Hearing this prompts me to go and ask one of the maintenance guys who is trimming a bush about thirty yards up from the apartment. He stops trimming as I approach. He has no doubt seen me coming and going from the dead guy's apartment. He realizes that I want something and looks at me cautiously.

"My friend, he live next door, he say he were shot in the chest and the neck," the maintenance man tells me.

Wow! Shot twice in the head, then stabbed in the chest "a bunch of times," then shot in the chest and the neck. Sounds like quite an ordeal. It's no wonder he died.

I become intrigued as I continue walking back to the apartment. How many different people will I have to ask, I wonder, before two corroborating stories emerge?

I go back in and help Jake pull the linoleum from the kitchen floor. He is standing in the kitchen, pulling at it, and

I am on the outside edge, levering it off the floor with a kind of shovel. The linoleum is stuck fast. Between us it takes a good ten minutes of toil and sweat to work it loose. The more we work, the more the smell thickens.

"Now it stinks!" Jake says as he carries the linoleum outside and places it in front of the door. "You watch," he says to me on his way back in. "The neighbors will be complaining about the smell within five minutes."

Jake starts spraying the kitchen floor with enzyme, making sure that all the areas where the blood leaked through to the floor get an extra dousing. He also sprays the bottom cupboards and the wall to be safe. He scrubs the floor and then starts to mop up the mess with tissue. I absentmindedly pick up an envelope on the counter, which is addressed to Eric Peterson.

"Do you think it's okay to use the toilet here?" I ask Jake as I slide the envelope back on the kitchen counter.

"I wouldn't, it's pretty foul-smelling. You could piss in it."

I stroll around to the bathroom, pulling at the buttons of my jeans. "Oh, motherfucker!" I scream upon arrival.

Jake is laughing when I come back around the corner.

"I told you!" he says.

"Jake, trust me your description of 'it's pretty foul' definitely falls short of the reality."

"I don't ever use the toilet where I'm working!"

Just then there's a knock at the door; the owner of the complex has stopped by to check on the work.

"Well, it's really been an easy job." Jake tells him. "The linoleum was so old and worn that I just pulled it up. Everything has been scrubbed and doused with enzyme. "

Before the complex owner replies, we all turn to face the front door, each of us having sensed a presence in the doorway. It's a young boy of about ten, twisting his neck at odd angles to see if he can see anything. He says something in Spanish and runs away.

"Well, it looks good to me," says the complex manager. "When you're done, drop the keys back at the manager's office and she'll sign your paperwork for you. Thanks for coming out so quick—the neighbors were starting to complain. See ya later, fellas."

"Do you know what happened here?" I manage to get out before he takes a step.

"Oh, it was nothing. He died of natural causes."

I laugh. I don't want to fall into Jake's trap of drug deals and drama, but the bloody body print that was on the linoleum floor suggested anything *but* natural causes. Any of the three suggestions given by the neighbors would in fact be more fitting with the scene.

"Yeah," the manager goes on. "He had hepatitis C. Apparently he passed out, fell, and cracked his head open on the floor and bled to death. He wasn't found for ten days."

I freeze from head to foot. There's no involuntary laughter sneaking out of me now. I no longer have any dumb-ass questions for the complex manager. Instead, I look at my minidisk recorder sitting on the kitchen counter. I look at my camera bag sitting on the floor just outside the kitchen area. I look at my camera sitting on top of the TV. (I hadn't actually planned on moving in, *honest*.) I look at Jake in his all-in-one protective suit and respirator. Then in a mirror I see myself, dumb-ass, wearing jeans, T-shirt, and an expression like my penis has just shriveled up to little more than a sun-dried raisin. I have had the knowledge of hepatitis C for only ten seconds and already I know I am going to die a slow and agonizing death.

I have heard of hepatitis before, of course, but in Denmark it has only started to get mention in the last year, and even then not much is being said. The truth of the matter is that we don't really know what it is. We have just seen ads depicting scenes of people holidaying abroad, eating and drinking in restaurants and bars. These happy scenes are followed by a warning against hepatitis and, more strongly, about bringing it back to Denmark. So, yes, I know it by name, and get that it is passed by body fluids. If that ad is anything to go by, you can catch hepatitis just by drinking from a glass previously used by somebody with hepatitis. And what is this C strand of hepatitis? Is it a supercharged version?

I find myself, without really having any factual knowledge of what hepatitis is or does, wanting to get out of the apartment fast. I mean, the guy living here *had* hepatitis, which makes his residence a stronger area of concern than the pretty little café in South America that was shown in the Danish health warning. I mean, who knows where his body fluids have been? I could have put my hands on the counter where last week he sneezed or spat. But the complex manager doesn't know that I'm a journalist; he has assumed that I am a cleaner. Shouldn't I be used to this kind of thing if I work with death on a daily basis? I decide that it's best to maintain my cover. But the complex manager should feel free to leave anytime. Sooner rather than later. I mean, has he not realized I have no further questions?

"I guess you guys see worse than this all the time, huh?"

Oh, *here we go,* I think to myself. Weren't you in a rush just a moment ago? Somebody around here must be late with their rent? Should you not go bang on the door? Collect?

I decide to nip the conversation in the bud. After all, I now have serious concerns about my health that need to be addressed severely.

"No!" I tell him. "This is pretty much as bad as it gets. The work we do really isn't as bloody and gory as people make out."

Jake allows me this and says nothing. The manager moves away and waves good-bye. I see him off the premises, little more than an inch behind him all the way. As soon as he is away up the path I gasp for air. You see, ever since I heard the word *hepatitis,* I have been trying to take as few breaths as possible. I stand outside, trying to retrace my steps.

What did I touch?

Where did I put my water bottle?

Did I touch the top of the bottle before I drank from it?

When will I lose control of my bodily functions?

At which point will I pass out and crack my head open on the floor?

Jake comes out of the apartment laughing his head off.

"Dude, you should have seen your face! Christ, it was just instant panic. I thought you were going to just turn and run. I really didn't think you were going to keep it together." He is almost doubled over.

But I am not laughing. I am certainly not keeping it together. What if I have contracted this hep C? What if, even after the televised health warning, I take hepatitis C home to Denmark, to my friends? All of a sudden the gift of transgender porn stolen from a dead guy is not looking as thoughtless as it once did.

"Alan," Jake says, sensing a panic attack to be imminent. "You're okay. You can't get hepatitis by breathing."

"Yeah, but—"

"Shit no! If someone with hepatitis sneezed on you, then be concerned. You didn't lick the linoleum while I was out at the truck, did ya?" Jake asks with mock severity on his face.

"What about if he sneezed on the counter, and then I touched that and somehow got bacteria in my mouth or something? What about my camera? He could have bled on the counter where I put it and now I've had it in front of my face—"

"Er . . . I don't know about that," says Jake, frowning. "But I'm sure you're fine. Don't worry. We'll clean it all with pure alcohol, *it'll be fine*. The chances are so small, but then if we clean everything, the chances are zero. Okay?"

I believe him, sure. But that doesn't mean I'm okay. Had I had forewarning, I would never have helped remove the linoleum; or laid my belongings down inside the apartment. I would have worn a protective suit and thick rubber boots, a respirator or three. In fairness to Jake, he never asked me to help. He also didn't know about the hepatitis.

Jake starts to bring my stuff out. I line it up on the pavement, holding everything at arm's length as if it's going to explode in my hands. Jake passes me a handful of cloths and some cans of 100 percent alcohol foam. I start with the minidisk, carefully wiping all the surfaces several times. I run a fresh cloth up and down the cable that runs to the microphone, spending a good two minutes on it. Once all the equipment is clean, I cover my hands and arms and rub vigorously. But my whole body is starting to itch, so I take my T-shirt off and cover my body in foam. Passersby point and laugh at me. Then they see that I am standing next to a Crime Scene Cleaners truck and stop. Jake finds this all very comical. But you never can be too sure, and I am not taking any risks.

"What happened?" one of the onlookers asks, grimacing at the thought of my answer.

Ears prick up all around. People shuffle and lean forward to better hear me.

"It's hard to believe," I tell him. "But absolutely nothing."

"Oh," a short man in jeans and a dirty white vest says with a laugh. "You got the heebie-jeebies?"

"Fuuuck yes!" I agree with a laugh of my own. *"The heebie-jeebies."*

I notice Jake throwing something into the back of the truck. It's the crime scene tape that was discarded by the front door. I stop thinking about hepatitis for a couple of minutes, because I realize now that it must have been the yellow tape. That must have been what had the neighbors speculating on the many and varied means of murder. When I spoke to them, none of them had gone over to ask the complex manager or the police officers what had happened. Otherwise they would have known that it was an accidental death. Instead, they had looked at the yellow tape and concluded that this tape spoke the facts. They read the tape as if it said "Crime scene, do not cross—deceased was either (a) shot twice in head, (b) stabbed twice in chest, or, (c) shot in chest and neck!"

How many people, when they say, "Guy across the street was murdered, it was drugs," actually have a factual standpoint for their statement?

"Basically," says Jake, "what the media has portrayed to society is that you see police, something has gone drastically wrong. They're like, 'Oh gee, something really bad has happened,' and then it's like . . . what's that game called?"

"Operator? Chinese whispers?" I ask as we drive away from the complex.

"Yeah, operator, that's it. As it moves from person to person the story changes from this to that. I find it amazing. Like right there, all the stuff you were told, and it turns out to be hepatitis. You know, they see the cops, the door all taped up. I mean that's what it is, you know, yellow, the color yellow. Primarily, the color yellow is used for caution. I mean look at all the stuff I was saying back there—I had him dealing drugs."

"Does it worry you at all, Jake?" I ask, shifting back to my own, more immediate concerns. "Hepatitis, AIDS . . . ?"

"Yeah! I mean in all honesty . . . I mean we're suited up pretty good. Each job's different but you have to apply the same amount of caution. Yeah, it worries me. Of course, I've got all the vaccines, but still. I bet if you were to go out in the street and ask a hundred people to come in here and do this job, tell them he had hep C and that there was blood on the floor and that he had decomposed, you'd get about two people out of a hundred that would come and do this job. You know, a lot of the time we don't know if these people had any diseases or not."

"Alan, I've got Neal on the phone. He wants to speak with you," says Jake, handing me the phone as he gets into the truck after stopping for gas.

"Hey, Neal."

"Dude, I hear you picked up hep C?" asks Neal, amused by what Jake has obviously told him. "Listen up, there's another job not far from you that Jake needs to get to quick, and then after that he's off to the jail to clean the showers where's there's been a bloody fight—"

"Neal, tell me I can go to the jail, please?" I almost beg.

"Dude, you can't. You have to be registered and I can't take that kind of risk. Anyway, I need you to help him 'cause he's short on time, okay? So get suited up and get cleaning, speak to you later, bye!"

"Neal, hold on a minute . . ." But Neal hasn't held on a minute.

"How do you find it working with Neal?" I ask Jake as I hand him back the phone.

"In what way?"

"Just his harsh manner, and the way he speaks to people."

"The way that he is to me is that he's one of those guys that's got little-man syndrome, you know. I mean he's a great boss to work for, he'll back you up, support you and get you jobs. He does all the hard work for sure; none of us technicians can do what he does. I mean he can close a deal by just telling people, 'This is how it's gonna be.' Either you go with it or you don't go with it. And he's got that Texas accent that he uses. He's not from Texas; he's from Capitola. In reality he's like a pimp, you know: 'You want him, this is how much he costs.' And he's got a good deal. Like I said earlier, go outside and find two people that want to come and do this."

"And they're probably already working for Neal."

"Right. It's one of those deals where it takes a special kind of person to do it, I guess, because most people don't want to—you're making money off someone else's tragedy, you know. I don't have a problem with it. But to have us do this, it really does help the grieving process, and then we make some money, too. We all win in the end. If that back there was a family dwelling with a wife and kids, and say the dad had been murdered, would you want the kids to see that? You walked in there with me; what did you see? You think the wife should clean that up? It was a body outline, you know, that's where dad was last seen, blood coming from his head. We help with the grieving process. We'll come in and clean him up, clean her up—clean *something* up."

At the next job we find ourselves at another apartment complex. We are shown in by somebody on the maintenance team who warns us that we are about to enter a bloody mess. He isn't wrong. The blood is spread out, trailing between the kitchen and the living room.

There are, of course, every year, in every part of the world, attempted suicides. Acted out by people who don't really want to die, but who want or need the attention. For right or wrong, they need somebody, maybe a parent or a lover, to look away from everything else in their own life and to look at *them*. Then there are people who truly want to die, but who don't succeed for whatever reason. There have been people who have shot themselves in the head and survived, sometimes even removing part of their frontal lobe with a bullet, but they didn't remove enough, and so . . . There are others who were found and were rushed to hospital and saved. But then there are those who want to die and who want to make sure they are dead. They do not want to be found and saved, and so take precautions against it happening.

This job appears to be one such case.

A man slit his wrists. Going by the amount of blood and the trail left by it, he spent some time moving around after cutting his wrists. There is a lot of blood in the bath and all over the bathroom floor. There's also a lot of blood in the kitchen, again all over the floor but also up on the cabinets. There's a large pattern of blood on the side of the fridge and dried-up pools in and around the sink. All this blood, for me, represents certain death. Surely you couldn't lose this amount of blood and survive? That said, this guy was found hanging from the light fixture in the bathroom.

I start work in the kitchen (fully clad, this time, in protective clothing), armed with a stiff brush, a pressure can of chemical enzyme, and several rolls of industrial tissue.

"Alan, it's pretty simple," says Jake. "Spray the enzyme on the blood, let it get to work. The blood's all dry and the enzyme basically just breaks the blood down, then scrub with the brush until there's no more dry blood, and wipe off with the tissue." Jake watches me as I apply a few squirts of enzyme. "You see." He smiles. "We're just glorified janitors, really."

I start with the refrigerator, pulling it out so that I can

get to the blood that has dripped down the side. I try to get a grip on the fridge without actually touching any of the blood. I am sweating as I jig the fridge from side to side. Swearing at the doors that keep opening with my efforts. I pull the right side, gain an inch, but lose half of that inch as I try to edge the left side forward. I am huffing and puffing and at best making half an inch at a time. But the farther out I get it, the easier it comes. Finally I put all my strength into it, drag it out with a screech, and notice that my hand and arm have smeared their way through the blood on the side. I am wearing the suit and protective gloves, but I had been hoping I could get through this task without actually touching the blood. I thought I could spray the enzyme from a distance and then use such a big clod of tissue that I would not actually get too close to the blood itself. Which is pretty optimistic, when you think about it.

Blood comes off surfaces like this, the fridge, really easily, which aids me in my attempt not to think about what I'm doing. The job isn't so much removing the sight of blood; it's as much about killing all the bacteria left behind. As Jake told me, the cleaners never know what illnesses the dead had when alive, and so removing all traces of blood and body fluids, with regard to health issues, as far as I am concerned, is a serious aspect of the work.

The fridge is clean in no time. I stand back and admire my work, wishing, given how easy the task was, that I had not been so keen. Out of the corner of my eye I can see the bloody kitchen cabinets and I know they will not be so simple.

The cupboards are old and very, very plain. There's no pattern or decorative styling at all. Just flat brown surfaces with small brass ball-like handles in the corners of the doors. There's little to no varnish left on them. When cleaning blood off kitchen cabinets I imagine you would appreciate some varnish. I know I would, because right now I am scrubbing and scrubbing, but the blood has soaked in over a period of days, and unlike the fridge I see little fruit for my labors. It's hard, sweaty work. Already I can see that it takes a very special kind of person to do this job. Not simply because of the ghastliness of it, but because the results of your grind often come at a slow pace. I can be spurred on if I see quick results, but this endless toil for such slow gains is thwarting my will to continue. And these are kitchen cabinets; it's not like I am working on a ceiling with my hands above my head.

Neal and his crew make it look so easy.

It reminds me a little of when I used to go around my neighborhood cleaning cars for pocket money. Sometimes you'd get a really muddy mess. Even then I never really had the staying power. I'd clean the parts you could see, but that was it. I was a surface man. I noticed after a while that I knocked only on the houses that had relatively new cars on the drive, because it was so easy to make them sparkle. Of course, this isn't a good target customer for a car washer. My earnings plummeted and I had to find another weekend job, one that didn't involve any kind of cleaning. The point here is, if I ever really made it onto the Crime Scene Cleaners team, I think Neal would fire me for shoddy workmanship in no time at all.

I am pretty exhausted by the time I have the kitchen counter free of blood. My hands are sore and cramping. I feel like that really should be good enough. But I can see around the sink, where the metal meets the counter, that there are still traces of blood. They are tucked right into the metal. Surely we should just pull these cabinets out and dump them? Can we really be expected to clean in these grooves? Would anybody notice if I just left them?

Luckily for me, I get pissed off. I grab a regular table knife from the drawer, wrap it in an enzyme-soaked cloth, and start scratching away at the blood around the sink. Sweat is dripping from my face, but I realize that this is the only way to succeed: to get angry, to allow myself to get angry.

Eventually I remove all traces of blood from the wooden surfaces. As I tackle the inside of the sink area—which, while I know it is going to be a simple job, is by far the bloodiest— I have the smell of blood stuck in the back of my throat. It's making me sick. I can't now help but think about the suicide, the person, the method, the pain, and I think that to do this job properly you have to just treat the blood as matter. You have to avoid putting a person to it. It can either be red (or quite often brown) stuff that you're cleaning, or it can be a person, the choice is up to you. But being new to this, I can't ignore it, so the choice is *not* up to me. Which is why I find myself doubled over and retching. The smell combined with my imagination is simply too much.

I would like, at this point, to offer some sound advice: if you are ever to contemplate such work, and you know you may, in the early days, be a little weak in the stomach, make sure you eat something beforehand. I mention it only because I didn't have the foresight to eat, and right now both sides of my neck are locked in jerking spasms that come in agonizing waves. The back of my throat is clucking and straining. My stomach seems to be fighting the urge to come flying out of my mouth, and this resistance is causing such muscle cramps that I feel I will soon have my first-ever six-pack abs. And my chest, why it feels the need to compete in this painful arena I don't know, but it's in there giving it everything it has. I sense that if this doesn't end soon I am going to tear a thousand muscles and cause myself permanent damage.

"Are you okay?" Jake asks, running into the room, his face expressing genuine concern.

I wave an arm at him and try to gasp some kind of communication between gags. I want him to know that it looks (and feels) more serious than it is. In reality, it is nothing more than an overzealous dry gag.

He stands there watching, seriously wondering if I am going to die right in front of him. His eyes light up for a minute and I realize that he is considering the Heimlich. I mean really? Can he believe that, surrounded by all this blood and horror, I have been snacking on the job here?

Finally the gag ends and I suck air back into my lungs with a loud wheeze.

"Dude, that was fucked up!" Jake says, as I lean against the wall and gather myself.

I am so relieved that I want to laugh. Yes, it was the most fucked-up dramatic dry gag in the history of dry gags. But I survived it and find myself overjoyed.

"I've opened the windows, but maybe you should just sit outside. I'll finish up," Jake says.

"No, I'm going to finish," I assure him. "I'm all right now. It's just, wow . . ." I have to stop for more panting. "Those dry gags are quite something."

"Dude, take a walk. Go and drink a soda."

My body aches. I feel like I've pulled several muscles. But Jake needs to be assured that I am okay, so I straighten up and try to get control of my breathing. It takes some convincing, but finally he lets me continue. After the sink there really isn't that much to do anyway. The thing most on my mind now is the awkwardness brought about by my vomiting. I try to cover the awkwardness up with the metallic sound of my brush scrubbing the inside of the sink.

"Why do you think you were sick?" Jake asks me, as we load up the truck and get ready to leave.

"It was the smell of the blood," I tell him. "It just got right to the back of my throat and I could taste it. I couldn't take it. I was thinking, *I have some dead guy's blood odor in my throat,* and that was it, I was off."

As I step out of my protective suit I notice that I am still a little freaked out by the taste of blood. It's not like I am going to break into a bout of gagging again. But I am still revolted by the thought, and will probably continue to be so for a long time.

"Dude," Jake says as he lifts the enzyme canister into the back of the truck. "Dry blood doesn't smell."

"It doesn't?" I ask, wondering if this is good news or bad news.

"I know what that was." Jake grabs the enzyme tank and drags it closer. He pulls off several squares of tissue and squirts the enzyme onto it. "Smell this," he says, wafting the tissue under my nose.

One quick, dry gag convulses instantly through my body. Still, I am a little relieved. It wasn't dead guy in my throat after all, it was the smell of the enzyme mixed with the tissue. It was this scent that led me into a fit of dry vomiting. Now I gag only once. Being aware that it's just chemicals, I am able to recover quickly. I feel a little stupid with this new knowledge, but happy at the same time.

It seems there is one more small job before we call it a day. Jake and I are off to the city morgue. To show the quality of the work Crime Scene Cleaners do, Neal has his staff clean several morgues every week for no charge. They clean off the gurneys and/or the insides of the vans in which the bodies are transported. They even clean inside the operating theater where the postmortems are done. Today, however, there's a high-profile postmortem (though they won't say who it is) being carried out and no unauthorized personnel are allowed into the operating theater. We will be cleaning only the gurneys: the tables on which bodies are stored and worked on. To do this, we have to collect some of them from the freezer.

The doors leading into the freezer room are electric. You stamp on a rubber pad in the floor and they open, you go in, and a few seconds later they close behind you. *Never* have I been so distrustful of electricity. When you are in a room with well over fifty pairs of dead feet sticking out from beneath cotton sheets, and your only escape is via a powered exit, electricity suddenly seems wholly unreliable.

The bodies here aren't stored in extra-deep filing cabinets like in the old movies. Instead, the entire room is a refrigerator, hence the automatic door that closes quickly to keep the heat out. Lined up on either side of the room are gurneys with bodies on them. You can't see the bodies, of course, just the cotton sheets and their feet. Some of these bodies have been in the morgue over a month. Sure, they're well cooled, but the smell of fifty decaying bodies, I assure you, is not something you want to be associated with.

"Now this smell is exactly what you think it is," says Jake. "And this isn't that bad; it's been a lot worse at times."

I have noticed that whenever I'm in a room where the odor of decayed human hangs in the air I try not to breathe. I take little sips as if drinking piping-hot coffee while standing outside in freezing temperatures.

In the middle of the freezer room, pushed up against one another at crooked angles, are the used gurneys that need to be cleaned. Jake and I start wheeling them out into the yard.

The gurneys are easy to clean. In fact, most of them don't even look dirty. There's the odd dribble of body fluid here and there, but for the most part it's just a case of dragging them outside, dousing them with enzyme, hosing them down, drying them, and taking them back inside, where they will await the future dead.

It's a smart move of Neal's, to offer this service for free. It's another way of getting the company name out there, and the work is easy.

Jake is keeping up his talk while we clean the gurneys. He is talking about some of the strong smells that have been here at the morgue. He is talking about a time when the freezer was overfilled with bodies. He also tells me about a mortician who works at this facility, noting for the most part her attractiveness. She walks around the corner a few minutes later. She is beautiful. Jake and I both straighten up, smile, and say hello. We come across as ridiculous and we know this because, while sweet about it, the mortician laughs at us.

"In our dreams," Jake says when she is gone. "Well, in mine. You'd probably do okay, being a writer and all."

"Hahaha, that's a myth, Jake. Everybody's a writer these days. We have become a common cliché and we're known for being notoriously poor."

"Yeah, but you're smart, you're intellectual. At least . . . that's the perception." Jake pauses. "I mean writers generally, I don't mean *you*."

Jake and I both burst into laughter as we stand outside in the sun. I am hosing down the gurneys, ridding them of their enzyme dribbles, and Jake is drying them with tissue. Aside from my jeans being wet from the hose spray, I am feeling really good. The image of Jake and me in this yard, surrounded by water spray and stainless steel gurneys that glisten in the sun, is one that will stay with me for a long time. I realize, as I laugh with Jake, moving from gurney to gurney, that this is as good a place to be as any. I am enjoying the work now. I am enjoying the company. If ever I find myself wanting to take a year out, to lose or find myself, I am starting to think that this could be the job. Especially now that I have cut my teeth, and got the vomiting out of the way.

A coroner's van pulls into the yard and Jake and I have to move the gurneys out of the way so the driver can back in, toward the freezer.

"There goes another one," Jake says, as we watch the back doors open.

Five minutes later we are back in the freezer, lining up the clean gurneys.

"Which one do you think is the new arrival?" I ask Jake, as we look at all the dead feet.

"Well," he says, surveying the options, "actually there's

a lot of fresh corpses in here right now, it's pretty hard to tell."

As the doors close behind us, on our way out of the freezer, we walk to the office to say goodbye, both hoping to see the beautiful mortician again. We do see her, and both dedicate too much time to smiling and waving before leaving the building.

In the truck, as Jake tries to remember where we left my rental car, Jake asks, "Are you sure you don't want to run in there and get her number?"

"Hahaha, you'd like that, wouldn't you? To see me crash on my ass?"

"Dude, just tell her you're a writer. Scoring chicks off being a writer isn't a myth; you're just trying to make me feel better." As Jake puts the truck into drive and edges toward the gate, he adds, "Remember, you're an intellectual!" and we drive off, leaving the morgue behind and laughing our heads off.

"Hey, Alan, it's Rachel."

Last year, when I was in San Francisco my friend, Rachel, gave me her apartment for a week while she was visiting L.A. It was a tiny, cold apartment with an overfriendly cat that I just couldn't find any love for. While I had told Rachel that I was coming back to San Francisco, I haven't actually found the time to call her. Now she is inviting me out to dinner with her and her boyfriend. I accept, of course, but have to warn her that should there be some kind of life-ending tragedy in any of the neighboring boroughs I'll have to leave.

She assures me that she understands.

In the shower I scrub every part of my body for longer than I have ever scrubbed before. I apply shower gel by the fistful. Once suitably raw, I get out, dress, and drive to Rachel's new house in Twin Peaks.

I love my job. I love traveling around writing articles, meeting weird and wonderful people. But it's moments like this that I like best, ones that really hit home how lucky I am. For me, there's nothing quite like driving through an unfamiliar city with a map wrapped around the steering wheel and a coffee in the cup holder. I love everything about it. I love being lost. I love darting onto the side of the road when I realize I am not where I'm supposed to be and need another, closer, look at the map. I love the cars that honk when I take a turning too late and cut off sharply. I like handling the map. I like the rustling of the paper as I spread it out. I even like the sound the map makes when I accidentally tear it in a bid to get it the right way around. The pen marks and the coffee stains made on previous jaunts are some of my favorite things. Running a red light and screeching to a halt because I was watching the map and not the road seems somehow thrilling, not stupid. I like the goose bumps. I like counting off the streets on the map as I go. But most of all I like turning a corner to discover that I have, even if in a somewhat roundabout way, successfully negotiated another trip.

Twin Peaks is a trendy, expensive district of San Francisco with a lively gay scene and a smattering of wine bars. As I drive through, looking at the many restaurants and bars, I remember from my research that this is the area where the man in the bath, Gary Lee Ober, used to hang out.

I wonder about the void left behind by those who are murdered. Because given a small change in the program, maybe just one coincidence less, perhaps a missed bus, they might not have been murdered. They could still be alive and well, doing what they would normally do. As I drive by I imagine the spaces in these local bars that are still allocated to Gary Lee Ober.

Turning right onto Twenty-fourth Street, I am greeted with one of those ridiculously steep roads that San Francisco is famous for. As this end of the street is quiet, I approach slowly, savoring the moment as I hit the incline at about two miles per hour. My weight shifts from beneath me and like an astronaut in a space rocket I am lying mostly on my back. In front of me I can see a young couple tackling this hill on foot. Instead of taking it head-on, they zigzag across the road from left to right, from right to left, increasing the distance covered at least threefold. They pant as they force their calves into the climb. Then they turn to me as I idle by, laughing at my two miles per hour as if I'm an idiot. I open the window to remind them that I'm not the one zigzagging up the street. But instead I ask them if they would like a ride. They jump in the back.

Acknowledging that this is the closest I will ever come to taking off in a rocket, I start to gather speed and enjoy a Thunderbird moment. Three hundred feet later my passengers get out and thank me for the ride.

A little farther up, I turn right onto Grand View Avenue. Just up on the right is Rachel's silver Beetle; beyond that, the road disappears into a steep decline. Her new house, which she rents along with four other people, is fantastic. Not least because it has a pool table, but also because it has a great mix of characters in there. There's a teacher, a dancer, and a community worker. Unlike in Walnut Creek, where my motel is, Rachel's roommates seem very real and down-to-earth.

We take Rachel's car and head out to North Beach for some Italian food. North Beach is a part of San Francisco that sits between downtown and the financial district. It's where the famous City Lights bookstore stands. The neighborhood is famous for being the nucleus of the Beat generation, which spawned such writers as Kerouac, Ginsberg, and Kesey. While those days are falling deeper into history, North Beach still has a vibe of something special going on behind every closed door.

North Beach is café society. Columbus Avenue is littered with Italian restaurants that look like they have stood there for decades. Most of the owners are outside trying to drum up trade—though I don't truly understand why, as most of the restaurants are seemingly packed. But still the Italian men stand sentinel to their establishments, singing and cat-calling to the ladies in a bid to beguile them through *their* doors.

Rachel steers us past another singing Italian man and through the door to his restaurant, Mona Lisa. There's a sign telling us that any customer who sings "Mona Lisa" all the way to his or her table will get a free glass of wine. But I am not often praised for my chirping, and pass the offer by.

As we sit chitchatting, waiting for our food, sipping our wine, I feel a little distracted. I am not taking every part of the conversation in and am worried that I might appear rude. But what is it? There's just something there. . . .

I feel relieved when the food arrives. Partly because I haven't eaten all day, and find myself ravenous, partly because it might help cover up my perplexed disposition.

David is asking me about my day, about why I am cleaning up suicides and why I think people might be interested in reading about it. I'm telling him about how I think death has been packaged in the media. About how the soap operas back home last Christmas were killing off all their biggest stars in bids to win the ratings war. How death has become chic and hairstyled and has morphed into the biggest sales tool modern culture has. I am telling him that I am working with Neal, that I am trying to discover whether he is a product of our death-as-entertainment society or whether he is defining it. Then I notice the hint of something malodorous in the air and look accusingly at Rachel's ravioli.

Is she really going to eat that? Should she not call the waiter over and demand an explanation?

No. Instead, Rachel pops a ravioli into her mouth and takes a sip of wine. I look at David. Shouldn't he stop her? She is his girlfriend, after all. They may not have been dating long, but from where I sit, the man needs to demonstrate some chivalry.

Then it occurs to me, as they go back and forth in conversation, even sample each other's food and offer light moans of approval, that they can't smell anything.

I look accusingly at my own plate.

My face twists and turns as my nostrils start to contract. Am I really the only one who can smell this?

Yes, it occurs to me in a thunderbolt flash. *I am the only one who can smell . . . who can smell . . . Eric!* Eric, decomposed body print on the linoleum, "hepatitis C you later" Eric!

I lean forward and sniff my risotto: it smells of Eric. I raise my glass of wine: it smells of Eric. As discreetly as I can, under the pretense of having an itchy nose and while waffling some rubbish about perverse intrigue, I poke my nose into my armpit. A charming dinner-table gesture, I know, but etiquette aside, guess who I smell? The waiter comes to the table to refill our water glasses. He leans over and I can't help but notice that he is wearing Eau de Eric.

I excuse myself hastily and dash to the restroom. First, I try to rid myself of the smell by blowing my nose. I take deep breaths as if I won't get any more oxygen for several minutes; like a freediver I suck the air deep into my lungs. I look at myself in the mirror, make eye contact, take a short run, and lean into the blow, raising the tissue and releasing my lungs through my nasal passages as if in some kind of tribal war dance. Pinch, release, pinch, release, twist, turn, stamp the heel and bow. I grab fresh tissue and have another crack at it.

But the smell seems to be getting stronger.

I run the tap and twist my head so that the water will run into my nose, being careful not to flood my brain. I insert tissues in my nose to dry the nostrils. Twitching like a rabbit, I test the valves. *It's better,* but I still smell Eric. So I smear some hand soap on the end of my fingertip and brace myself with my other hand on the sink. I know this will smart, but still, it has to be better than having a dead guy in my nose. . . .

I am glad to report, back at the table with a concerned-looking Rachel and David, that I no longer smell Eric. But then again, nor can I smell my risotto, my wine, or, in fact, anything what-so-bloody-ever.

Job done.

We spent about an hour and a half in the restaurant, heartily covering many topics. But now, as I drive home, I think about nothing but Eric and the fact that I discovered him in my nose. Of course, it was the decayed version of Eric, but it was he, and it was probably the last time he would have an olfactory impact on another human being. It was one thing to leap around the restaurant toilet like an idiot, trying to rid him from my nose, but right now I am struck by his being there at all. It's as if he wanted to be noticed one more time, it was his last chance to commit himself to a memory. It's clear that Eric and I couldn't be further apart: I am of course alive and well and he is, one hopes, resting in peace. On the other hand, we were in that moment linked to each other, joined together by his last odor. Sure, as he left the stage he was no bunch of roses, but the fact that I was the last to carry his scent feels truly significant. I feel like I was a stage that he stood on as he concluded his last act.

Neal is so often the final curtain on the people he cleans up. How many times over the years has he been the last point of contact? It's an odd relationship Neal has with the dead. They leave their final mark on the world, and for those who commit suicide, leaving that mark is often a conscious wish. Then Neal comes along and removes all traces of it. He is working against them for the most part, but what he is doing in that final moment is incredibly intimate. His work is the last physical contact the deceased have with this world. The interaction they share is on the limit of human experience. It may not look that way as he sprays and scrubs and sings his songs, but Neal is exposed to the parts of people that nobody else (barring a surgeon, maybe) has seen. Those who choose to die seem to serve themselves up; it is the ultimate offering: here I am, my every thought, desire, and wish is now plastered on the wall, *enjoy*. But Neal is the one who actually gets up close and personal with that gesture. He is the one targeting all those dreams and depressions with his putty knife. He is the one seeing them off the premises, as it were.

If there is an afterlife I wonder how these dead souls feel about being ushered off by such a man as Neal. If you went out with a big gesture, hoping for maximum impact on a lover or family member, only to be greeted by a singing stranger wielding a putty knife, it would be fair to feel a little cheated. It would turn your grand exit into a bit of a farce. Life's last joke delivered by the fact that somebody simply must mop up the dead. People can't be expected to live around the mess, and so out of a basic necessity Neal Smither arrives on the scene.

But should somebody in Neal's position behave differently? Can they be expected to tiptoe around the dead? To care? Surely not. If crime scene cleaners felt anything for the dead they clean, they would not last but a few months in the job. To tiptoe around death, they would have to more candidly acknowledge their closeness with it.

Even so, I don't think Neal's behavior and antics are thoughtless. At the same time as drumming up media attention, he is self-protecting. His songs are a buffer against the fact that he has somebody's brains on the end of his scraper.

For me, having met Neal and having spent time with him, even coming to respect and like him, I can't see how it should be anybody else in such final moments. If I were to one day find myself dead and splattered against a wall, I would want it to be Neal who came to scrape me up, and if not Neal, somebody very much like him. *Don't cry for me, crime scene cleaner!* Just do a really good job.

THE CAVALIER MAN

Neal and I are driving around town in an erratic manner. He has chores that need doing: mailboxes that need emptying, invoices that need sending, and checks that need to be deposited in the bank. Even though there is no immediate rush, Neal still darts about like a man very short on time.

"Wait here, I'll be back in a minute," he says, as he jumps out of the truck to post his mail.

He strides off at a pace in his red Crime Scene Cleaners T-shirt and beige shorts and disappears into the post office. A few seconds later he bursts back out into the sunlight. He jumps back into the truck and starts the engine quickly, causing me to wonder if he has just robbed the post office.

"You know, I got sick once, don't ya?" he asks as we pull sharply away from the curb. "Oh yeah, I got *real* sick once. I thought I was going to die. And in the last week I was really starting to get my head ready for that. I lost thirty fucking pounds in a month. *Thirty,* dude, and I don't have that much weight to lose."

"What was wrong with you?"

"Never did find out. The day I was to have a liver biopsy—you know what a liver biopsy is, right? It's where they take a piece of your liver out and test it. That's serious. That's *real* serious! My liver was shutting down. My liver and my spleen grew enlarged. Fuck, I was sick, dude. I was living on Gatorade for *three* weeks. I was sick for about a month and a half."

"Do you think this was something you picked up on a job?"

"Oh, I know *the* job I got it at."

For some bizarre reason, Neal goes quiet. I don't know why. I sneak glances at him to see if it is an emotional story, to see if the fact that he nearly died catches in his throat even today. But it doesn't look like it. He turns the music up and starts singing.

"Neal?" I call out over the music.

"What's up, dude?"

"What about this job, the one where you got sick?"

"You wanna hear about it?" he says with a smile, and this time, without missing a beat, he continues with the story. "Well, I was in Vegas. We had press. There was a documentary crew with us and I was just, you know, too cavalier about it. I went in there without a respirator on and the lady had died of liver failure. There was urine everywhere. I mean, everywhere. Dripping outta the mattress. *Pouring* outta the mattress! And I fucking inhaled that shit, man! And I got sick the next day. The next day I couldn't eat. My last meal was like, lunch the day of that cleanup, and I didn't eat another meal for about forty-five days. I couldn't eat. I couldn't make myself eat, my body just wouldn't take it in. But I could drink Gatorade, so I was drinking gallons of Gatorade every day. It was the only thing I could keep down, and man, I dropped weight. I fucking dropped some weight. It scared the shit outta me. And I was *sick,* my body was just *sick.* I couldn't do anything. One week, I can remember, I was sitting in my chair and the phones were ringing and I just did not give a fuck! And man I *always* answer my phones. I didn't care. I let 'em ring. I was hurting. I went to the hospital and I had so many tests, I had so much blood drawn. I had colonoscopies done. I had MRIs done. I had CAT scans done. And then the ultrasound that they do on the women, I had that done, too. They just could not figure out what the fuck was going on. They kept asking me, 'Are you drinking? Are you drinking?' I don't drink! *I don't fucking drink, man!* My enzyme counts were all off. It scared the shit outta me! That last week I said, 'Fuck, I'm dying.' So I started getting ready for that 'cause I didn't know when, but I was sick enough that I thought it was going to be soon."

"What do you mean you were getting ready? How did you get ready?"

"Just mentally, I started to get ready for it. Started to figure out what I needed to do for Lyndey. I was scared. I was really scared. And then, *dude,* one day, I woke up and it was like I had never been sick. I felt—"

"Hungry?" I laugh.

"Well yeah, I ate that day. And I didn't eat a little, I just *gorged* myself. But there was nothing. I mean I felt weak, of course, but the sickness was totally gone."

"Did you go mad? Were you just running around like a madman now that you were better?"

"No. I was in shock, I was scared, like, 'It's gone into remission. It's gonna come back.' So I slowed down a lot."

"So, how quickly did you get back into work?"

"Oh, *immediately*! I had neglected everything for a— *Oh, look at this asshole!*"

I am trying to see what asshole Neal refers to, but I can't stop laughing. It's typical Neal: "oh, I slowed down all right—*to about two hundred miles per hour.*"

"What asshole?" I ask.

"The fucking asshole behind us with red and blue lights on his fucking head. This son of a bitch is gonna give me a ticket. You watch."

"License and registration?"

Neal says nothing, but hands over his documents.

"You know these windows are too dark?" the officer asks.

"Yeah, I do, but . . . You know . . ."

"Well, if you know already, why have them? You're getting a ticket."

"Yeah, I always do."

"You always do? When you get a ticket you have to have the tint removed, then get the ticket signed off to state that the tint is gone. Or at least within regulation."

"Oh, I've done that many times, officer."

"So what? You go get it put back on again? Why would you do that? You like paying the fines?"

"I like paying the fines a lot more than I like people staring at me all day, hell yeah!"

"Well, here you go. Have a nice day now."

"Dink!" says Neal as we drive away. "I'll set my fucking . . . Mormon friends on you, *asshole*."

"Who are your Mormon friends?" I ask as we get going again.

"They're my friends, dude. I gave a talk to them two nights ago. They wanted me to talk to their leaders about what I do and what it costs."

"How did this come about?"

"Well, the motherfucking Mormons have been knocking on my door for like *a fucking year*. 'Good afternoon, sir,' and all that. And one day I got to thinking, the Mormon organization is worth fucking billions, *I wonder how these boys like their coffee*. Of course, they don't drink coffee, but I invited them in all the same."

"And what, you're going to join them just to get their business? You're now committed to the sectarian dollar?"

"Alan, don't mock it. Do you have any idea how much money the Mormon organization is worth? Shit, I kid you not. If there are other religions out there that I can potentially make money off, damn, I'm signing you up. I'd get you room and board at Jonestown if it were still around."

Neal and I drive along, laughing. I am wondering if Neal really would sign me up to a religious sect, but going by the expression on his face, he is not considering *if* he would sign me up to a religious sect, but *which* religious sect to offer me to first.

"Hahaha," Neal breaks out in giggles. "You'd look real cute as a Mormon, Alan."

THE DARK LORD PERFORMS A JEDI MIND TRICK

We are on our way to Richmond to price up the clearance of a garbage house. You have more than likely seen them on TV. They pop up now and again in films and docudramas. Whenever there's a need to portray a local nut whom all the kids in the neighborhood are scared of (though there's always one little fat kid who pretends not to be scared in order to win some kudos), the hoarder in the house full of trash and cats is a character often opted for.

Garbage houses with lost and forgotten, sometimes crazy, sometimes just old, proud and lonely people inside litter every state map in America. Cleaning garbage houses after the long-forgotten occupants die and decompose in their beds is a big part of Neal's business.

As we arrive at the house, the owners, or at least the very, very new owners—the ones who flew in from out of town to organize the clearout and the quick-as-you-can sale of the house—are waiting for us on the driveway.

The windows have all been boarded over and the front door fitted with new locks. The new owners won't be going into the house with Neal and me. They say the smell is too strong.

Such houses are called garbage houses not least because they are full of garbage; it also has a lot to do with the fact that the garbage is arranged exactly as it is on a garbage dump. It's as if somebody plucked the roof off and then an oversized truck came along and dumped the garbage inside the house. It's packed in really tight. It even looks like it's been bulldozed into position, but of course it hasn't. This is the human hand at work. The plastic bags are piled up high and mixed in size and color and contents, exactly like at the local dump. Actually, now that I think about it, I think I know what happened here. The occupant, while out for a stroll one day, saw a nice garbage mound and decided, to save on time and labor, to build a house around the mound itself. The only thing this enclosed dump site lacks is several hundred scavenger birds circling and squawking above. There are living things circling, though they are not squawking. They buzz and fly at face height.

But the smell is of greater concern and importance. I follow Neal through the house wondering how long I can hold my breath for. I haven't forgot his "I nearly died" story, and I am not wearing a mask.

In the first room there is a bed piled high with garbage bags, blankets, magazines, bottles, letters, and empty air-freshener cans. On the other side of the mound is a dressing table, still equipped with beauty products, which are covered in dust and cobwebs. There is also a TV. The standby light glows, but the screen is a mass of dust. More cobwebs hang between the television and the wall. It's as if the occupant got bored and stopped living in the room one day without as much as a glance back as he or she started tossing garbage in there.

The kitchen is an abominable mess. Here the occupant decided to dispense with the formality of garbage bags. Sauce bottles, drink cartons, food packets—just about everything you can imagine—have been tossed in here loose. Flies flit back and forth, hopping from plastic bottles to empty cans. I am not convinced that they are going to find what they want anymore, but they show no sign of giving up.

The smell is always there, but sometimes it manages to get deep down in the lungs. My stomach gags. I have to go back to holding my breath if I want to keep my latte down.

The bathroom is the only room that has been kept free of debris. At least the occupant realized that human waste should be disposed of in the traditional manner. But this room, while free of empty ketchup bottles, is still rank. It's like something you might expect in a film about people left to rot in dank, infested prison basements.

"Alan, keep it in!" I hear Neal say over my shoulder. "Dude, you can't throw up here. Hold it in. Hold it in. Alan, *concentrate* . . . Hold it in!"

Neal sounds like a counselor as he coaches me through the process of not vomiting. Still, it works. It does take several gags before I have myself under control, but I do get the better of the reflex. The problem is that there are six other rooms to inspect.

Neal reaches all the rooms ahead of me, kicking doors open on arrival. They are all jam-packed. I don't want to go into the rooms anymore, so I just peek in through the doors.

I have the feeling that it will never end, that as we continue down the twisting hallway, pop in and out of rooms, we will always be greeted with more doors and, hence, more garbage.

Even the hallway is packed full of garbage, scum, and flies that send me skittering about in my bids not to touch or tread on anything. But this garbage, it's not all food cartons and sauce bottles. Jutting out at odd angles are signs of life: an old clock, a jacket, a birthday card. There are signs of a life lived here, but where there's space for a human being to have lived in it I don't know. I can't even begin to think where this person slept.

In one of the last rooms, I find out. On a small tan fabric sofa, opposite a television, are the body fluids of the recently decomposed. This room is deep inside the pit. Whenever this person went to the toilet, opened the door, or pretty much did anything, it would have involved quite a trek from this room, through mounds of garbage and clouds of flies.

Back outside, on the driveway, I want to fall to my knees and drink the clean air. But the clients are waiting for us there and so I put on a brave face and try to maintain my calm.

"Okay, we're looking at—at least six large Dumpsters here."

Neal begins to tell them what is needed and what the cost will be: "I'll put four guys on it and it will take two full days. It's going to cost you about forty-five hundred dollars. Now you don't have to answer right away. Like I said, my name is Neal. I'm the president of the corp. You need anything, you just get me on the phone."

For a minute it looks as if Neal is going to walk off. Does he want the job or is this part of another Jedi mind trick?

"No," one of the women says quickly and firmly. "We want you to do it. We want to get the house on the market. Can you do it this week?"

It strikes me as a little odd that the two women are so well groomed for this occasion. Their clothes are well made; gold brooches and diamond rings sparkle in the sunlight. Their hair is styled in big dramatic balls. You can't get your hair buffed and buoyed up like that without professional rigging, specialist tools, and a team of trained assistants. It is clear that they both have visited the hair salon recently, I would even go as far as to say today.

And why not? I suppose. Maybe they are going to a party after. Maybe they didn't know their relative was dead and they just popped around to pay a surprise visit on their way to a gala. You could hardly expect them, on finding the dead relative, to turn to each other and say, "I don't know about you, but I feel a little overdressed."

"How does Wednesday grab you?" says Neal, making me jump, making me realize I have been staring at his clients. Even though I turn away, I am still focusing on them. I can't picture the relationship between the two women before me and the person who must have lived in this house. Where do they connect? Two are overly turned out to meet a crime scene cleaner and the other was living in foul conditions.

"Oh, that would just be great," one of the women says. "I am so grateful to you, you don't understand."

"You bet. Anything of importance we find we'll put to one side, any deeds or money."

"You will? Because we caught one of the neighbors in here. We think they were stealing money."

Neal is on the phone as we drive away in the truck, but

he is paying enough attention to notice that I am once again about to vomit. Without discussion or signal he pulls sharply into the edge of a grass verge. I open the door, lean out, and throw up. He hands me a tissue while still on the phone. I lean out, gag once more, and wipe my mouth. Neal starts driving off while the door is still open.

"Dude, if I was that way inclined," he tells me as I close the door, "I could've hit her up for another grand at least!"

I start laughing immediately. Neal thinks I am laughing at his words, but I am not. Are there to be no inquiries into my well-being? I was only hanging out the door being sick, after all.

I feel sad about the situation we left behind. Why are the family members there so quickly after death when there is a house to be claimed, and not when there's a life to claim? It's very easy, of course, to sit here wiping vomit off my chin while rewriting somebody else's life, making decisions based upon my empty conclusions. Maybe there are a thousand valid reasons why. But still, at this point, with a body stain on a sofa, a house full of garbage, and two well-dressed and at times embarrassed relatives on the driveway, it is cutting and depressing.

"Why did you say that about finding money? Is it normal to find money in such places?" I ask Neal, wanting to get away from my thoughts.

"Fuck yeah. You gotta understand, these people are old. They all lived through the Depression, where all the banks went belly-up. These people lost their houses, their savings, their *lives*. So they don't trust banks. So yeah, in houses like that where somebody elderly has died, you generally find a lot of cash, or lots of bonds. We found like twenty grand in one house just like that, just envelopes everywhere full of cashed benefits and bonds. It was just so much money. Did you hear she said they thought the neighbors had been stealing? That's common, too. Neighbors get in there and pretend to help, maybe they go grocery shopping for them once a week, but really they're just robbing them."

"Why do you think people choose to live this way? Buried in their own garbage, I mean. Do you think they are mentally ill and should be in a home?"

"I don't think it's a choice as in A-B-C. Some of them are mentally ill, but, dude, often it's because these people are just proud fucking people. It's pride that gets them in this mess. They get old and eventually they can't contain themselves and they don't want people to know. They don't want people to see them like that. They're too proud to ask for help. They lose their grip on the house, can't physically cope, but they wouldn't dare call anyone in because they don't want to be dependent on anybody. They don't want people to know that they can't cope. Then the place gets to a point where they're too embarrassed to let anybody in. Before they know it, they're completely bedridden and that's that.

"I am not going out like that. I hope to raise my boy to be a good person. I just can't believe people live and treat each other the way they do. I mean family, you know?"

"Does it make you sad, seeing these things all the time?"

"I don't really think about it like that. I mean, when you ask me directly, yeah, of course, but day to day—I just think about how many Dumpsters I'm gonna need."

"What about situations like the one we just left. They seem quick to move when there's a house up for grabs."

"Alan, you haven't seen shit. For some reason, a lot of

these people become adversarial with us, and it's generally not the people that we've had contact with to schedule and all that. That person's generally too distraught to deal with it anymore. So we have to deal with the idiot relatives who for some reason make us the enemy. They're fighting for belongings and they don't want us there to hear it. They're just not good people. They're dirty, filthy frigging animals with no sense of courtesy or decorum, you know? 'Dude, your grandma's spot is on the floor. Fight over the belongings when the janitors have gone, okay! I mean God Almighty. You haven't seen her for at least thirty days. She was on the fucking floor, dead! So how the hell do you know that she wanted you to have that bureau, like it's your fucking birthright?' "

"Sometimes, Neal, you sound like you really do care. You get worked up."

"No, I don't give a shit. That's not the way my life is. They choose to live that way, man. I mean mentally, absolutely it affects you, but what? Are you gonna let it eat you up, or are you gonna make your life better or work not to be that way? I couldn't live the way most of our clients live. I just couldn't do it. I really just could not fucking do it."

"Do you think you would feel that way if you had a regular job—like in a bank?"

"No. Probably not. I'd just be going along like everyone else. But with this job you are confronted by death every day, and you are confronted by how people treat each other every day. It's an eye opener. You get to see how the loved ones behave once you're gone, or behind each other's backs. It changes you. But I'm a pretty driven guy anyway. I mean, once I have it in my head as a goal, I have to achieve it or it's gonna kill me. Mentally it will eat me alive. It's like, I have a certain money goal right now and I swear to God it's all I think about all day long."

"That's pretty sad, too, Neal, to be so driven by money."

"Oh absolutely. It *is*. I know"

MAN IN THE BATH PART II:
I KNEW YOU WERE COMING

I am up bright and early this morning. I sit drinking coffce and reading continually in my attempt to keep my mind free from death. But there's no point, really. Soon enough I have to get back to it. Soon enough I find myself driving through the city, wrestling with my map as I realize once again that I am on the wrong street going the wrong way. For a second I am tempted to keep going the wrong way, to drive away from death. But I don't. I turn as soon as I have an opportunity and get myself back on track.

The Superior Court building in San Francisco holds the courts, jails, and the police departments. It's a busy building, and at this time of the morning most of the people are going in. I am greeted by a metal detector, uniforms, cheap suits, and a continuous hum of noise.

I make it up to the homicide division, where I sit waiting

for my appointment. The space in the reception area is small, crowded in by black office furniture typical of cheap 1990s furnishings.

There are officers, wearing varied shades of beige, standing around talking about a baseball game that's coming up. Some have big bellies. Others have big mustaches, something that, I am told, represents authority. The mustache being authoritative is the biggest Jedi mind trick the world has ever seen.

Aside from the officers all flicking their eyes at me (it's a little comical; as if they are trying to figure which murder I am here to confess to.) and giving me the once-over, the atmosphere is what you would expect in a *normal* office setting, not a homicide division.

I am here because I am following up on the story Shawn told me about the man in the bath. I want to know what the police were doing while Shawn was up to his elbows in Gary Lee Ober.

"Hi, Alan. I'm Inspector Joe Toomey. My partner will be with me in a second. Can I get you a coffee?"

Inspector Joe Toomey is a big, broad-shouldered fellow with a very friendly face. He is wearing a beige suit with white shirt and a blue tie. His silver-framed glasses work their way into his silver hair. He has been on this job for around twenty-five years, but he doesn't look hardened or traumatized by it. I am sure he acts otherwise when necessary, when dealing with a murderer, but straight off the bat he seems like a really nice guy. As I am led into an interrogation room I am introduced to Joe's partner, Inspector Holly Pera. Judging by the look she gives me, I realize that either Inspector Pera does not have time for me or she doesn't like journalists.

Holly Pera is slim, with long dark hair that nestles on the shoulders of her dark blue suit. Like Joe, I am guessing she is in her fifties. She seems much sterner than Joe; her expression is tight-lipped, but of course this could be for any number of reasons. But for sure she doesn't take fools gladly. It is impossible, when looking at the inspectors together, not to think of good cop/bad cop. I am glad to report there is not a mustache between them.

It's very odd sitting in this small room. On the desk is a tape recorder that, for a change, isn't mine. On the wall is a clock. Apart from that, the room is void of objects. There's just my good self and the two homicide inspectors who sit opposite me, looking patiently at me, waiting for me to speak. I wonder what it must feel like being brought in here as a criminal. It's an odd enough feeling being here as a journalist. I can't help but be aware of the fact that the people in front of me have been dealing with murder/murderers firsthand for more than twenty years. How many times have they sat there, where they are now, and looked into the eyes of murderers? How many lies and tales have they heard?

The look on Pera's face has me thinking, *Have I murdered anyone lately?* I am getting the impression that one wrong move on my part and I could be up before the judge in the morning, which leads me to explain what I am here for.

"I am interested in a case you worked about a year ago," I begin. "The death of a man called Gary Lee Ober. I believe a man named Jim McKinnon has been charged with his murder?"

"Well," says Pera, eyeing me suspiciously, "what is this for?"

"I'm writing about a company called Crime Scene Cleaners and they cleaned up the scene where Gary Ober was found dead. So I am just looking to get some background info on the case."

"And this is for publication when?" Pera asks.

"Well, it's for a book that I haven't started writing yet . . . so a year and a half by the time it's available, at best."

Holly Pera has a skeptical look on her face and I totally understand. I think it's probably the look most journalists get from Holly Pera. Hearing my own words, I can see why one would be suspicious, or possibly appalled. It is, in its basic form, pure voyeurism. It must be frustrating at times for homicide detectives to have so many people fascinated in them for what they do. They are themselves, by association to their job, a "morbid fascination."

I show Pera a letter from my publisher that seems to validate me on some level.

"How did you come to be looking for Jim McKinnon?" I ask, hoping they can't read my mind.

"Well," begins Pera, "We had the name 'Jim' from a neighbor, because the man just happened to introduce himself to a couple of neighbors by that first name. We were told, by his very good friend that lives across the hall from him, that Gary frequented certain establishments down in the Castro district in San Francisco, which is the predominantly gay district: a lot of bars, a lot of restaurants, clubs. And so we," Inspector Pera signals her partner with her arm, "went down there to the bars and ran into, really, *the most helpful bartenders,* and so a number of them, you know, listened to what we were looking for and one in particular and then two and then three said, 'Well, we know that there's a guy named

Jim that knew Gary and his name is Jim McKinnon. And he's kind of a homeless type and he was staying with Gary for a little while; we don't know where he is now.' So that's how we got onto Jim McKinnon."

"What was the next step? Did you then go about finding him?" I ask, a little taken aback by how much Inspector Pera has said in answer to my first question.

"We basically put the word out on the street and we also put a Teletype out saying that we were looking for this particular person. We began to hear that he might be staying close to the Hall of Justice here in one of the, like, daily- or weekly-type hotels. So we tracked him down there, I think it was Twelfth Street, wasn't it, Joe?" Inspector Pera asks her partner.

"Yes, it was Twelfth Street."

". . . And interviewed him in his hotel room and then brought him down here and interviewed him some more and then arrested him. I guess it was about a week in all."

I can't help but notice that as Inspector Pera has been talking, a large smile has spread over Inspector Joe Toomey's face.

He leans forward in his seat a little. "He sat right where you're sitting now," he says with a point of his big hand and a sparkle in his eye.

For some reason, the idea of my sitting in the same seat as a murderer sat in throws me a little.

"Really?" I ask, fidgeting uncomfortably.

Now Inspector Pera is smiling, too. "And as soon as we met him, he said, 'I knew, I knew, I knew you'd be coming, I wanna tell you what happened.' He said he'd been in a fight with this man. He said there'd been some pushing and shoving but he said that he never used a knife. He didn't really deny killing him, but he didn't admit it, either; he just admitted to being there for an event that probably caused this."

"Did what he was telling you match up to the scene or the evidence?" I ask.

"To a point." Now Inspector Pera has a frown on her face. "We believe that Gary was stabbed and he will not admit that there was a stabbing. He also mentioned to other friends of his, this is Jim, mentioned to other friends of his that he'd killed somebody before and there was some mention of baking soda and other things that go along with what we know about the scene."

"See, the thing is that, the . . ." Joe Toomey pauses and looks at his hands, unsure of how to continue. "The condition of the body . . . do you know anything about that?

"I know that it was pretty unpleasant," I tell him, earnestly.

"The body was found in the bathtub," he continues. "It was almost like a skeleton. That's all that was left—"

"*Gel!*" interjects Inspector Pera.

". . . And from the neighbors we knew that this *Jim* had been staying in the apartment within days of the police finding the body. So what you do know is that this Jim has been in this apartment for a month or three or four weeks, with a dead person, right? So, I mean, that's what gets you onto Jim. There's no way that Jim can say that he didn't know the guy was dead. I mean the owner was . . . You could, you could . . ."

Inspector Pera finishes the sentence for her partner: "You could smell it down the street. Literally, *down the block*."

"Seriously? As you approached the building, you could smell it?"

"Oh, *down the block!*" Inspector Pera almost shouts. "Several houses away you could smell it."

When they talk about the case, the inspectors appear rather animated. Two things are very clear: first, that this, even for two inspectors with decades of experience, was a very bizarre case; second, that they *are* their work—being a homicide detective is not something they do from nine to five, it courses through their veins twenty-four hours a day. You could be mistaken for thinking that they are talking about a case that they worked on a week ago, not a year ago. They are not searching for the details, the details are right there, at the front of their minds.

"This was the worst." Inspector Pera stops to clear her throat. "This was the worst smell I've ever . . . This is the worst one I've had, I mean in terms of smell."

"See, don't forget, it was confined, too." Inspector Toomey looks at me as he says this with raised eyebrows that say, *You hadn't taken that into account, had you?* "You know, if this is out in, say, a park—the body was dumped— he's got open air. First of all, it was confined to a bathtub in a bathroom, and that was also in an apartment that was closed—you know all the windows were closed."

"The guy put the heat on," Pera says with genuine surprise still in her voice. "He was trying to speed up the decomposition process."

"Then the bugs started to come from the apartment," Toomey says, and as he does, as I realize that my head has been flicking back and forth between the two inspectors, I notice that they are enjoying themselves, too. They are enjoying the storytelling process as much as I enjoy it. "Not just the odor that the other people in the condominium are smelling, but the people living below it—the bugs from the body started coming down into their apartment."

We're getting to the part that really interests me now; this is the stuff I have not been able to fathom.

"Did he say anything about the fact that he was living in this apartment for a month while this person was—"

"Oh no, and we didn't either," Pera says, cutting me off. "No. And we certainly weren't gonna act like that was bizarre because I didn't want him to read something from me and think, 'I better not say anything about this, the police are gonna think it's crazy.' I was just like, 'Oh,' and we just went right along with what he said."

"So he openly admitted to living there all this time?" I ask, amazed.

"Oh yeah, staying there!" Pera corrects. "He tried to say that he moved out a week before we knew that he had, but even then! I was like, 'Oh, okay.' You know, even then it would have been just awful."

"Yeah, 'cause when the different neighbors had asked him where Gary was, didn't he say Gary had won a cruise and he'd be back in seven or ten days?" asks Toomey, turning to his partner. "I forget exactly what time frame he said. But when that time frame had expired and they'd asked him again, 'Where's Gary?' and he'd come up with . . ."

" 'Oh, I was wrong,' " Pera mimes. " 'He'll be gone another week.' "

"Was he relaxed or nervous?" I ask as I try to picture him sitting in this seat. "Or was he scared when you brought him in?"

"As soon as we hit him with the tough questions he started singing," Pera says, making her partner chuckle.

"He really kind of put on this big act like he was crazy. Joe and I have interviewed many crazy people and it's just very different when they're really crazy, versus when they're putting it on. And he just sang and pretended like he was crazy. Basically he was just trying to screw with us is what he was doing; it was a game. And he was just trying to wear us down a little bit and we just weren't about to be worn down and we finally just got tired of him after a few hours because it wasn't going anywhere. We got what we wanted; we got as much as we were going to get."

"Enough to arrest him?" I ask.

"Oh, absolutely!" Inspector Pera fires back assuredly.

"Oh yeah, he started pontificating," Toomey continues, still with a little chuckle, "a lot of various things around the world, and then after an hour or two he goes, 'Well, you guys are gonna have to leave,' and we kind of said, 'Oh, okay, but you're coming with us!' Then we brought him down here, and since he was now in custody we had to give him his rights and we did give him his rights and he was sitting in the same chair you're sitting in and he started singing 'Amazing Grace.'" Toomey stares at me with raised eyebrows and a puckered face. "A little off-key, I might add!"

Laughing now, Pera continues, "But you know when he said, 'I'm expecting you. I was expecting you,' we said, 'Well, you know, Jim, we just wanna talk about what happened, you know?' And he immediately went into making admissions, saying that he had been seated on the toilet, this man had come in, he'd been staying with him for a few days, the suspect wasn't feeling very well, he was on the toilet, and the victim came in and wanted him to orally copulate him. There was a little pushing and shoving that took place and that's as far as he would go, you know, 'pushing and shoving.' Guy ends up in the bathtub, is what he tells us, and that's that, that's it, that's as far as he'll go. He denies that he used a knife on him. When we confronted him with more evidence about that, and the fact that there are, you know, knife marks and things, he just starts singing and carrying on. In that chair!"

Being told that Jim McKinnon sat in the very same chair, the one that I sit in now, keeps making me jump. A part of me doesn't want to hear mention of it again. But at the same time I have to fight with my face muscles to stop a smile spreading. I think the inspectors are playing with me, trying to give me an attack of the jeebies. But they are too late for that. Or, they're going to have to try much harder.

"You see, the problem with killing someone in your own home," Toomey continues, sounding a little bit like a teacher, "is what you do with this body. And in this case, his mistake was that he stayed there. See, he should have left and then, whether we would have known who it was or not, you know, would he have had that much contact with the neighbors? But see, what people don't realize, when you kill somebody in your own home or a home that you're gonna stay in, the big problem you have is what do you do with the body?"

"That's a big issue!" Pera adds.

"With the evidence as it stands," I ask, "is it strong enough to convict Jim McKinnon?"

"Aaaaaaaaaah!" says Pera as she sits back in her seat and removes her hands from the table.

Now this is a long *aaaaaah!* and it makes me sit up straight. I wasn't expecting an *aah* of any length. I was expecting, "Oh my God, yes, have you not been listening? He was living with the dead body!"

"I would say," Inspector Pera continues, "that it's going to be difficult to convict him, say, of a first-degree murder, or maybe even a second-degree murder, and that is because the body was so badly decomposed and there are no other witnesses and it's *this* guy's word against *this* guy's word. But you know, is it likely he'll be convicted of some sort of a killing even in a jury trial or plead guilty? I think it is. Yeah, *oh yeah*."

"He has a couple of options, you know?" Inspector Toomey adds. "His attorney could also enter a plea of insanity. Not guilty by reason of insanity."

"When you said earlier that he started singing and acting crazy, it made me think that maybe he had an insanity plea on his mind right from the start. Do you think people get such ideas from TV shows?" I ask.

"I think a bigger problem," Joe Toomey says, shifting in his seat, "is that the *jurors* look at the TV programs and they always think there's gonna be so much physical evidence, DNA and all this stuff. But you know, most of the time those things aren't there. It just doesn't happen, you know?

"Ever since the OJ case everybody thinks that DNA is all over, and you know, sometimes it doesn't amount to anything. Especially if the killing happened, say, in your house, and you're the suspect or you're the victim. I mean, your DNA and stuff is supposed to be there."

"The other thing jurors don't take into account is money," points out Pera. "It costs a tremendous amount of money to run a DNA test, it's a couple of thousand dollars every time.

So, we don't always run DNA tests because we don't have the CBS budget. So if there's other ways to prove it, then we're not gonna run a test because we don't have enough people to do the testing and it's very expensive. But the jurors see it on TV all the time and so they expect it. So when the defense attorney says, 'Inspector, did you test this or that for DNA?' and you say, 'No,' then the defense attorney raises his eyebrow like, 'Aha!' "

"So the attorneys are actually using the influence of entertainment knowingly?" I ask. "Because the attorney works cases all the time, right, he knows how it works? I mean, the attorney will know why the test hasn't been done? The funding constraints? Or the suspect having lived in the house et cetera?"

"Oh, they know," Pera says with a flick of her head. "Because they themselves can request that evidence be tested. I love it when the defense attorneys do that to the jurors. They say, 'The inspectors had every opportunity to run the DNA to prove that it could've been somebody else, but they didn't do it."

"And!" Inspector Toomey almost shouts, "if they don't have any money to do it, the city has to pay for them. What Holly said was right, about whether we do it or not. But if the defense wants it done and they don't have any money, the city *has* to pay!"

I sit quietly for a minute, pondering the game. The way people's lives hang in the balance of other people's understanding of the game, or the skills with which they play it. I don't mean just the lawyers, I mean the people who commit the crimes that result in their needing a lawyer. We seem to live our lives and make our decisions based on personal risk assessment. That could be an assessment of whether or not we will be able to pay the mortgage this month if we book a vacation. It could be about speeding on the highway when we're late for work, risking the chance of getting pulled over and being fined, not to mention being even later for work. It could be about having an affair or slitting somebody's throat because he or she looks funny.

"Do you think the value of life is slipping?" I ask.

"Hmmm . . ." Inspector Toomey pauses for a moment. "In the areas of these gang killings, it seems like the homicides are . . . almost happening on a regular basis, you know, they're becoming . . . *common*. They have no respect for anyone else's life. They have very little respect for their *own* life. They commit these killings and ten minutes later they've forgotten about it: 'it's no big thing, we're playing the videogame now.' "

"But there is so much of it on TV," adds Pera. "There's so much discussion of it in rap music and there's so much of it in some communities that those living in the middle of it all are a little desensitized. I think it's . . . *yeah,* and I think it's really sad. Every TV show has somebody dying. Every murder show and every time you turn the TV on, whether it's some gangster show or whether it's a *Law & Order* type of show, it's death, death, death, death, death. Death's not as horrifying as it once was. What Joe and I have found in some of the rougher neighborhoods is that when we go *knock, knock, knock, knock* on someone's door to tell them that, you know, 'your son's been killed,' or whatever, they're sad, but they're not surprised! They know it's gonna happen, and the young people figure that just a couple of things are going to happen to them, these are the only choices when they grow up: they're either gonna be killed by the time they're probably twenty-five or they're gonna have to, quote, 'go sit down,' which means go to jail."

"Holly and I had a case," Toomey says, leaning on the desk, "where a young guy, about eighteen or nineteen, was found with his face half shot off with a shotgun and another shotgun blast to his back. He didn't have any identification on him, and he had never been arrested, officially arrested. If he'd been arrested we have everybody's prints. So there wasn't anything, but he did have a tattoo on his arm, *Rest in Peace So and So,* with a name and a date. We looked it up in our files and it turned out that that person was also murdered. We got that old case file for, how many years prior?" Joe asks his partner.

"About six years."

"And we went out to that victim's mother's house . . ."

"Hoping that she could tell us all the different people who put tattoos on their arm," Pera adds.

"Oh, and it's only about a block and a half from where the second homicide victim was found. And she told us one person and it never fit the description. We go, 'Anyone else?' And she said, 'Well, my other son.' And so we go, 'Well, may we speak to him?' And she goes, 'Well, he didn't come home last night.' And then we asked, 'Does he normally carry identification?' She goes, 'Yes, he does, but he didn't bring his wallet out with him last night.' Well, we borrowed the wallet, and in California—when you get a driving license—they take a fingerprint. So we had them fax the fingerprint from the Department of Motor Vehicles and it turned out that it was her son."

"Her *second* son," Pera says, looking down at the table.

"Her second son was murdered, too," Toomey reiterates. "So there are some mothers, some mothers in these gang neighborhoods, that have a number of their children murdered."

"And you know, it's what we were saying." Inspector Pera sighs as she looks at me. "They don't seem to be too terribly surprised. But it would be so easy to say it's all a part of their community, they're not that terribly affected by it; it would seem as though the males are not that affected by it in terms of how it affects their mood and everything. They just kind of grow up to think this is what they're gonna do. But the women are so depressed. The women are so depressed and Joe and I see this all the time. In their day-to-day life they're so depressed and so worn down and I just really think it is this, it's living with this. You know, it's a very unnatural thing to have this happen over and over again. But they don't realize it's unnatural because it's their life. It affects them by making them very, very depressed, and where it affects the males is by being more aggressive. I think.

"But I also think that . . . Like years ago, when I first came into the police department, you were just starting to see guns. It was more knives; people would beat each other up. Now, guns are *so* accessible to these young people. They're coming in from foreign countries. I do know from research that they're coming in from just a couple of different places, China, Mexico, and our government is working to try and curb that, back in China and back in Mexico, to stop that. 'Cause it's only a few different places and they *need* to stop that 'cause all these kids have guns. Everybody's got a gun, they don't go out for dinner without a gun, they don't go to a club without a gun, *everybody*'s got a gun. So it's just so easy, and the other thing is, years ago, these people that were selling drugs were not using the drugs themselves. They were just selling them. Maybe they'd use a little marijuana just to chill out or whatever. But now they're using the drugs and they're using drugs like ecstasy and some of these other drugs that make them *very* paranoid as time goes on. And they're mixing meth and ice, you know, and heroin and then the crack, and so it just makes them terribly impulsive, terribly paranoid, and then they have access to guns."

"But they don't care about anybody or themselves," Toomey adds.

"Oh, *that's* a huge thing too, yeah," Holly agrees. "But they've got the tools."

It has been interesting, as the inspectors have told their stories, to watch how they have gone from being animated about a single case to exasperated about the overall picture.

"How does it affect your outlook on life?"

Nobody says anything for about half a minute.

"What a good question . . ." Pera says, breaking the silence.

"You know, sometimes you make comments," Toomey begins. " 'Jeez, this is sad . . .' but, I don't know. . . ."

"It depends on the case," Pera adds. "I think it depends on how innocent the victim is. That's really hard when it's an innocent victim, someone that really did not deserve it. But then the flipside of that is, even the people that aren't innocent victims, it depresses me a little bit, it frustrates me a little bit because the system is just so out of control, it's so out of control. I don't know what the answer is, you know, I don't know whether it's just swifter and more severe punishment. But how do you get back and change this mindset from so many years ago. It's so frustrating. I really do feel bad for a lot of people that are in these really repressed communities, because they live in the housing projects, which is very, like the outskirts of town, they don't ever get outta there. You know, their life is different in there, they don't see anything any different. They don't have the opportunity to. They're usually fourth and fifth generation now; people living there have never had jobs. I guess they try to make a difference in the schools, you know, to try and encourage these children to go to school, that they have other choices, but the peer pressure is so strong and their world is so different. We can't even begin to shovel sand into the tide; we're not even at the beach! Hispanic communities are the same—crazy, crazy killings because you're wearing green and Joe's wearing blue and you're on his block and he's on your block, I mean it's just *ridiculous*." Pera is genuinely frustrated, gripping and releasing her hands as she talks.

"Yeah, actually they're the most stupid ones . . ." Toomey agrees.

"It's over nothing! It's so sad!" Pera says loudly.

"But there are also good people in these communities," Toomey adds on a lighter note. "It's just that they're not out at three in the morning when the drive-by shooting takes place. They're asleep! So we don't get to meet them."

I say good-bye to the inspectors and begin my exit through the corridors of the superior court. I am surprised by the inspectors. I was expecting, after all their years of experience dealing with death and murder, to find two people very desensitized to it. But instead what I found were two people clearly affected by death, and the stupidity of the common themes that lead to homicide. I found two people who care not only about the outcome but about why it happens. I feel reassured by these two wonderful characters. It's fine that they have no solutions, nobody has, but the fact that they have a heartfelt reaction to what is happening on the streets leaves me with some kind of hope.

DEATH AND DAYS OFF

As I am still half obeying European time, I awake at six A.M., full of the joys of a sunny Californian morning, wondering what awaits me. What bloody bedlam will I get to document today? What ludicrousness will Neal offer forth?

But Neal isn't picking me up until eight thirty, so I lie in bed with CNN. I am aware that I do not have a healthy relationship with the news. I feel that news is so very important, and am often moved by the idea of recording factual content, and see it as quite a special and important art form that should be respected. For me, the news should be without interpretation—no, strike that, it *has* to be without interpretation. What is needed is a factual rundown of the day's key events. What news channels should be providing is unmeddled-with recordings. History. Commentary is great, but it is not fact; it's opinion and therefore should be part of another format. And so I get myself in a lather when the news anchors relay a story with a little too much canned emotion in their voices, and then turn to their colleagues and start sharing their views on the matter. Shut up! You're a news anchor, relay the facts and move swiftly on. It's a horrible trend, this opinionated news, but I guess at some point I will have to accept, as it spreads around the globe, that the news has lost its original function of simply keeping us informed. Now the news organizations think they have to give us our opinions, too. It's like listening to a bore in a bar. It's low-level entertainment, a service industry, and like all good service industries it is serving up what the people want: death in large portions—death-as-entertainment.

I turn the TV off, take a shower, and go out for breakfast. If I am going to have to listen to other people's opinions on noteworthy events, I'll do it in a café, where the opinions are at least of the people and not scripted to capture the wider demographic.

After breakfast, I pull back into the car park of the motel and notice Neal's truck poised in the corner.

"Dude, you're cool. Go take a shower!" are his first words to me as I open the passenger door. "I need to make some calls anyway."

"What do you mean, 'Go take a shower.' I've taken a shower," I say, sniffing my armpits.

"Oh, okay. No problem. I saw you drive in and I thought maybe you were just getting home. I thought maybe you got laid last night."

"I've just been for coffee."

"Okay, well let's fucking go then. Get in the truck! Damn!"

As we drive, Neal tells me about a meeting that he has set up with a guy from Utah who wants to open a Crime Scene Cleaners franchise. He will pay Neal a lump sum of money and trade under the existing Crime Scene Cleaners standards and name.

"Do you have many of these franchises set up?"

"Eighteen, nationwide. I'd like to get a few international ones, too. If you wanted to set up in Denmark I'd invest in that. You could clean up in Denmark. I hear they like killing themselves over there. But really, I'd like to get a few more set up in the U.S., just to give our national contracts—like our motels—better coverage. But frankly it's a pain in the ass. People don't wanna work; they want everything for free. Then they get it and they still don't do anything with it. You know, it costs me money to set these fuckers up."

"So you don't make anything out of the fee?"

"After the lawyers and contracts and meetings . . . not really. I just don't wanna shut Utah down. It's been open six years. But you have to sell there; if you don't sell, you're outta sight, outta mind. So, I guess I could move to Utah, but I don't wanna do that."

"What's in Utah, anything?"

"World-class skiing and outdoor stuff. But I don't care about that. Frankly, man, I just wanna play with my baby, love my wife, and make money. That's all I wanna do and I wanna do it here."

At the office, Neal is expeditiously writing out invoices for the work that has been completed in the last few days. Even with invoicing, everything is fast, fast, fast. He sits like a student in an exam, bent over the pad, almost as if he is protecting his answers from straying eyes. It sounds like an exam, too, the way Neal's pen is busily scratching its way across the invoice pad, a sound that is now and again broken up by the ring of Neal's phone.

"Yeah, yeah. Compliment me some other time, motherfucker!" says Neal as he hangs up the phone and moves on to the next invoice. "I know I'm good, but can I go now? Jeez! Okay Alan, I'm done for the day. It's nine fifteen. Wanna get some breakfast?"

In typical Neal fashion, we screech up outside a diner and park on the red tow-away line. Before I can even point this out to Neal he is out of the truck. I realize, of course, that there is nothing to point out. He knows exactly where he has parked.

"Aren't you worried that you'll get towed away?" I ask his back as he enters the diner.

"Nah, they won't touch my truck. People love that truck, except the neighbors—they try to tell me that I have to park it outta sight, so I tend to park it on the street as much possible."

"You like to engage, huh?" I ask Neal, laughing.

"Not really. My neighborhood's full of old fucking people. They wanna golf. This is like their fourth or fifth house that they're retiring at. This is my first house, dude! I'm not stopping here. I may keep the house 'cause the appreciation is incredible around here, but I wanna live on the fucking Carmel coast. That's where I wanna live. Those are six-, seven-million-dollar houses, and so I gotta work!"

"Wow! A lot of people need to put their brains on the wall for you to buy one of those houses, huh?"

Neal laughs. "Fuck yeah!"

"Keep scraping!" I laugh.

"But you know, I'm a phenomenal saver, dude. I can save some major dough."

"Do you ever get into it with your neighbors about . . ."

"Fuck yeah. *Yesterday*!"

"What happened?"

"She came up my driveway, looking at everything. I pull onto my driveway, I'm like, 'Can I help you?' She's like, 'No!' 'Then get the fuck off my driveway, lady!' She started getting rough with me. I just told her, 'Lady, get your big fucking ass outta here!' But the truck is the biggest issue. You know, if the truck said ABC Construction there wouldn't be an issue, so fuck 'em, man! They don't look at the fact that I'm thirty-four years old. I'm half their age and I live in one of their houses."

"Do you really think that's part of it?"

"I don't know. I think they're just blinded by the 'crime scene homicide suicide' thing. They think I'm some kind of freak, you know. But I am really boring. I mean *really* boring. If you weren't here I'd be at home right now playing with Jack, picking flowers, you know, sitting on my porch not bothering anybody. I want privacy. Leave me the fuck alone. If the truck said 'Bio-hazard Cleanup' there'd be no problem, but because I'm more assertive with the marketing . . .

"I just don't take any notice. My truck's not going anywhere. When I first started, I used to have my big white truck, like my others but the big one. And I used to do all the work, and if I had an especially funky load in the back, I used to pull up next to people at the stoplight with their windows down and watch them. Or I'd race to catch up with a convertible so that when the light turned I'd be next to them. It used to make me laugh so hard! 'cause you know, they smell it, and they're like, 'What the fuuuuuuck?' And then they turn around and they see me laughing my fucking head off. Then they read the side of the truck and they're trying to get their roofs up and they're flapping and shouting. Fucking funny as shit, man. But the neighbors have nothing to complain about. I have never brought a load home and I never will. Not even passing through."

An odd thing has happened since our arrival in the diner. I thought I was imagining things, at first. I mean, it has to be a coincidence. It can't be because of . . .

"Oh, God, the place empties out when the Crime Scene Cleaners come in!" the waitress says as she comes to our table with pen and pad in hand.

So I am not the only person to notice. The diner was a little over half full when we entered, now it is empty except for Neal and me.

Were we that loud? Are people scared of catching something? Does Neal's close relation to Mr. Death cause people to run for the their lives?

"I'll take the Jimmy Ds with eggs over easy, a large coffee, and a large glass of milk," says Neal, clearly not interested in the departure of the other customers. "I can't wait until Jack's that age," Neal says, referring to a boy walking by outside. "I just can't wait to take him places with me and . . . teach him, you know? My dad was a failure, dude. He never did any of that shit, plus, he was just a failure, period."

Neal freely admits that he views every phone call as a moneymaking opportunity. Yet, every time the phone rings he complains and throws his cutlery down with a clank. "Damn, man! I'm trying to eat my Jimmy Ds!

"Which city and state, sir? Okay, well, look, I can get her there anytime you want . . . aha—aha, well, everything is guaranteed. If you see anything you want to raise, my name is Neal, I'm the president of the corp, you just get me on the phone, we work for you. So please, anything at all, just get me on the phone. Thank you, sir, thank you, you have a nice day now." The very second Neal ends the call he looks into the phone, as if the phone has eyes, and tells it, "Fuck offff!" Neal loves it when his phone rings and he loves telling it to fuck off if the phone call didn't evolve into several thousand dollars.

"Fucking guy. Has us come out and clean where a guy took his own head off with a shotgun and there's one light! One fucking half-watt bulb and he's like, the next morning, 'I found a speck of blood.' No fucking shit, dude. No fucking shit you found a speck of blood. If you only have half a watt of light tell me and I'll bring light! I don't mind buying you a fucking light bulb, you cheap ass motherfucker! Just let me know, okay! I mean, what do you think I am? A fucking owl?"

After breakfast Neal drops me back at my motel. There are no jobs right now and Neal is going home to play with Jack.

Walnut Creek, where I am staying, is a dull, Bermuda Triangle of a place. Soon after the departure of Neal I find myself immensely bored. But with crime scene cleaning being as sporadic as it is, I don't want to drive anywhere in case a job comes in. So I have to stick around. To grin and bear it.

COOLER THAN ELVIS

There is no trip to the office for Neal this morning. It is Saturday, and so I must sit and wait for the call. I do most of this sitting and waiting in Starbucks, reading Martin Amis's *The Rachel Papers* and drinking too much coffee.

I call Neal, just to confirm once again that nothing is happening. He assures me he'll be on the phone as soon as anything comes in. I cross the road, murder a burrito, but soon find myself turning numb. Walnut Creek is killing me. As the neighborhood is little more than an outdoor shopping mall, my options are limited. I hurry once again to the cinema for cover. But I don't want to watch movies. I don't want to be in Walnut Creek. I want to be working. I want to mop up the dead. But it would seem that death is not a well-oiled machine and I am noticing, on just the second day without any crime scene cleaning work, that I am starting to feel frustrated by this. It comes like a passing reflection in a mirror, an angle of yourself that you haven't seen before and that you really don't like.

After the movie I drive over to Neal's house. One of the cable channels is showing a documentary they filmed with him six months ago and we are going to watch it together. The house is silent when I get there. Neal motions for me to be quiet, Jack is asleep. The television is turned down low; we sit and watch the documentary without talking as the screen flits from job to job. It's typical Neal on the screen. He doesn't tone himself down for the camera, but then he doesn't tone himself up, either. The only time Neal speaks to me is at the end of a clip where he has just cleaned up a homicide: "Damn . . . I'm cooler than Elvis!" he says. Then, turning to me, he adds, "Okay, Alan, if anything comes in I'll get you on the phone."

Right you are, I think to myself. *I'll be off then.*

I scurry out as quickly as I can.

SELLING TO THE FUTURE DEAD

The past two days have yielded a zero body count. Now, here we are on God's day of respite, but what I want to know is will the devil also be resting on this here Sunday?

It seems so. All I have done is drink coffee and eat pancakes. Now I am back in my motel room, sitting on the bed, reading a brochure about cryonics. A while back I visited a cryonics facility in Arizona. I guess it was my first direct foray into death. I brought the brochure with me, thinking I might go back for an update, to see what part cryonics is now playing in our death culture.

Originally, I was interested in doing a story on them, but felt so cheated by the place that I never really got around to it. I drove twelve long hours through the desert, barreling along at speeds I really shouldn't have been playing with, and when I eventually I found myself in the storage room of the Alcor Life Extension Foundation, one of only two facilities in the

USA that deals with cryonics, I wanted to get in my car and drive back to L.A.

Before me stood some very normal-looking metal cylinders with stickers on the sides. This was the "patient care bay." I was terribly disappointed. I went there expecting images of science fiction. I mean, we are dealing with future innovations here; why can't the visual elements be designed to match the perception? Far be it for me to say, never having been a Trekky, but stickers just aren't very futuristic. They lack galactic quality.

Not for the first time, Hollywood had farted in my face. Where were the flashing screens? Where were the unexplainable oddities oscillating at the speed of light? The dials and glass viewing panels for keeping an eye on the subjects? The dry ice spewing across the mezzanine floor? The hyperdrive? I wanted some Hollywood, some cool visuals and far-out technologies. But in reality there wasn't even a button to push. In fact, the Alcor patient care bay, if anything, was suggestive of days gone by, not some futuristic vision.

For three o'clock on a Tuesday afternoon the building was surprisingly quiet. Like the rest of Scottsdale, Arizona, it looked like it was built just five minutes ago. Speed-dried by the intense desert heat. The building was basically two huge cement blocks that stood two stories high, separated by a slope-roofed entrance. There was something very eerie about this building from the outside, with only a few cars dotted around the large car park.

There was simply no sign of movement.

Nobody coming.

Nobody going.

It was pretty much the same on the inside. There were no

white coats gliding along the corridors. No prospective customers. No deliveries. No regular employees. There was just Paula Lemler, my tour guide for the afternoon. But maybe that was to be expected: this wasn't after all a high-turnover business.

There's a lot of skepticism about being stored at low temperatures (vitrified) after death with a view to being brought back to life in the future. Alcor themselves admit that right now this isn't feasible. But then, at the same time, they don't believe you are dead just because your heart has stopped beating.

"We're not there yet," Paula Lemler told me, "but we will be. The way science is progressing, the day will come when we will be able to restore life. Maybe that's fifty years away, maybe it's three hundred. But I, and everybody here at Alcor, truly believe in that day."

Their pitch is based on scientific breakthroughs that thus far don't exist. But they are confident that one day, maybe after a cure for cancer is found, they will be able to revive one of their members and exercise such a cure on them. At the outset, I have to agree, there really is little to lose. The worst thing that could happen is that you will remain dead. So, if you have the money and the desire, it may well be worth humoring science.

But there are just so many questions. First up (call me defeatist), I would need to see some radical improvement in human behavior before I ever thought this planet worth a second stint. If I could be packed off somewhere else, never heard of, never seen, for better or worse, it would be worth a gamble. But the way planet earth is going? No, thanks! The only reason would be to see how the kids are doing. But what if you don't come back for two hundred years, which from where we stand now would appear an optimistic time frame. The children will be long gone. Sure, one would hope for a generational trail, but what are you going to do? Knock on the family home and announce, "I used to live here!"?

Can you imagine the scene? In-laws can be troublesome enough. Some couples find it hard enough to accept each other's parents in the now; imagine if said parents were several hundred years old.

The chances of your actually being wanted in three hundred years' time are slim. Sure, you'll be wheeled out at first for cocktail parties and after-dinner speeches, but what of you then? Once the novelty value wears off, you'll be cast aside like any other aging fool. Only it will be easier to dispense with you because nobody will have any emotional connection to you. You never bounced them on your knee or took them out for ice cream. For the last three hundred years you *were* an ice cream. All you did was thaw out one day and turn up.

What other reasons could there be for coming back? A loved one? You could be vitrified together. Return together. But most people can barely keep a marriage together for one lifetime. Two lifetimes of marriage to the same person? There would be no surprises left.

There are many myths about cryonics: first, that it's called cryogenics. Cryogenics is the study of the cause and effect of extremely low temperature. Cryonics is the study or practice of keeping a newly dead body at an extremely low temperature in the hope of restoring it to life at a later date with the aid of future medical advances. I know this because the Alcor Life Extension Foundation brochure is kind enough to point it out.

Another myth is that cryonics is expensive. And yes, to you or me, $150,000 may be a lot of money. But, you can actually pay for the procedure with life insurance. All you do is take out your policy and name Alcor as the legal benefactor of the policy, so in reality the cost can be very little. There are even entire families who are members; mum, dad, and the two kids. The people of Alcor foresee a future where cryonics is a natural choice. Instead of being buried or cremated, it will be just as natural to be packed into an arctic cylinder full of liquid nitrogen.

It is generally accepted by the cryonics societies and newsletters available on the Web that "rebirth" will not become an actuality for several hundred years. My opinion is that unless cryonics specialists start thinking before they speak, it will be several hundred years before people start taking cryonics seriously, let alone being reborn. This opinion, I should alert you, is based not on any scientific fact or reasoning but on reading through the booklet "Alcor Life Extension Foundation—An Introduction by Jerry B. Lemler, M.D." The booklet is packed with credible titles, filled with Ph.D. Tom and M.D. Harry. But there are also some alarm bells that ring loud. The first is the reference to Alcor members as "Alcorians." I am not about to accuse Alcor of being a religious cult, but surely anybody alive in the last thirty years can name a few that sound uncannily like "Alcorians." I mean come on, add "ians" to the end of any word and you have taken your first step toward founding a cult. Try it. See, you're a cult leader now.

To put such an awful tag on the membership really discredits everything that Alcor might be about. To me the tag suggests that they are aiming themselves at sci-fi fanatics and or other assorted nut jobs.

Dr. Lemler, in his booklet, is quick to list his acquainted Ph.D.s and M.D.s. But from where I sit, it doesn't take an eight-year education to realize that by calling your members "Alcorians" you are begging to be harangued and mocked. Ever since coming across the phrase I have found it hard to come to terms with Alcor as a professional organization.

There are other interesting uses of Ph.D.s in the brochure.

"Eminent Extropian Philosopher and Alcor Member Max More, Ph.D., uses a compelling analogy involving an automobile," writes Dr. Lemler:

> If we say a car has the capacity to move at 110 mph, we mean that it is currently in a state such that, given appropriate stimuli (such as gas, a foot on the accelerator etc.), it will achieve 110 mph. The objection claims that we don't mean that the car could achieve 110 mph given available technology, and we don't mean that, given some empirically possible but non-actual technology, the car could achieve 110 mph. The problem with the objection lies in the fuzziness of the terms "capacity" and "appropriate stimuli."

Mr. Eminent Extropian Philosopher and Alcor Member Max More, Ph.D. (who with such a name could also moonlight as a porn star and/or trusted name in news anchor), goes on for many paragraphs in the same vein and tells us . . .

well, *nothing*! What he does do is use an awful lot of words to promote his branch of the death industry. He tries the old bamboozle technique. Say it, say it again, and again, and then slip in an analogy that, well, by the mere fact of its being so incompatible with what you're talking about can't really be called an analogy at all. He talks of disconnected wires, about how capacity can be restored by reattaching the wire. Sure, but how many human beings have you seen in the street immobilized by a loose wire? But the analogy gets thinner. What if the car is broken and there is no current technology that can fix it? "Further suppose that the manufacturer tells you that they are working on a new repair process that will restore function, a process that should be available a month from now." Yes, I can "further suppose" until the cows come home, I just can't get myself to further suppose all the way to accepting that that a broken-down car is in anyway comparable to a dead body. Mr. Ph.D. rounds up with. "The car analogy, then, supports rather than undermines the case for basing a criterion for death on irreversible loss of capacity rather than currently irreversible loss of capacity."

Seriously!? Appropriate stimuli indeed!? If the "problem lies" in the "fuzziness" of the terms "*capacity*" and "*appropriate stimuli,*" Mr. Eminent, I suggest you don't use the terms *capacity* and *appropriate stimuli,* they were, after all, if I am not mistaken, your own words.

It's an overused and overrated technique, to try to sound so smart, hoping to make your reader feel so stupid that what you are saying will go unquestioned.

THE NOSE HAIR: I want to sound smart when I talk. Would you help me?

THE BRIAN: Well, that's easy; first off, give yourself some grand title, like "Extropian." All you have to do then is stop midway through a sentence for effect, hold your pause with words like *such that* or, my personal favorite, *appropriate stimuli,* and talk around in circles without ever really getting to a point.

No, I don't think I will be going back to Alcor. It's not that I don't believe that the service they offer will one day become a reality. I do; I hope so, at least. I just don't like the way they sell death, or nondeath, to the dead. I much rather prefer Neal's death economy, which, by the mere fact that Neal's customers are generally not viable for cryonics, underlines the necessity of his existence.

For those of you, however, who are interested in cryonics, I suggest visiting cryonicssociety.org, a Web site that seems to give the subject the proper respect. But that's for another day. The last thing I want Californians opting for today is cryonics; what I need is more along the lines of mayhem. I need Neal to call me with another job.

SELLING TO THE RELATIVES OF THE DEAD

I am heading into San Francisco, but this doesn't mean that the drought on death has come to an end. Far from it. But instead of moping around worrying about the progress of my book, and generally praying for death, I've decided to cheer myself up with a visit to a funeral home.

Inevitably, in the midst of all this, I have begun to wonder about my own death. How will it come about and when might that day be? The more I see of it, the more certain I become that I will never commit suicide. As I now live in Denmark, where very little happens in the way of crime (at least when compared to the UK or the USA), it is very unlikely that I am going to be murdered. I no longer drive. In Copenhagen we tend to mince around on our bicycles. I haven't heard any news reports of six-bike pile-ups claiming the lives of all its riders. The odds that my death will be a natural, gray-haired, toothless, and incontinent one are wonderfully high. So what then? What are my options once I have filled the bedpan for the last time? I am expecting to find the answers at the Halsted N. Gray Funeral Home.

Before I go any further I will just say, to give you a little more insight into my character, that I have very few problems with spending money. Which . . . well, there is a problem in that I generally don't have that much, but still, I am happy to spend, spend, spend. Take Apple computers for example. By my own standards, I am truly amazed that every time Apple comes out with a new laptop I am quickly able to identify (in my mind) a real need for it, as in the case of the recent European launch of the new MacBook Air. Which is odd as my existing MacBook is but six months old. But you understand, I can't fit my current model into an A4 envelope, hence I have rather successfully established the "need."

Anyway, the point of this sideways ramble is that it takes very little to get me to draw, sword like, my wallet from my pocket. If the salesman is capable of forming words, I'm buying, baby.

So here I stand in the showroom of Halsted N. Gray Funeral Home, agog, as I stare wide-eyed at what is, one day at least, a purchase more necessary than any other I have ever made. I am not agog because I am faced with a technological wonder. I am not in awe at the way caskets have developed over the last few decades. I can't, for example, slide one into an envelope. I could, though, given the size of the casket that stands before me, throw a party in one, but that only begs the question, *Why would I?*

Why, then, does my jaw refuse to close?

It's because (and this is one of the few areas where Apple

could learn a thing or two) sitting on top of the casket is a little beige card that in a gold serif font informs me that the casket, the thing that will one day contain a dead body and be buried out of sight and smell six-feet-under, actually comes with a twenty-five-year guarantee.

Splendid! *Wrap one up!*

A twenty-five-year guarantee? Of all the incentives to attach to a casket, this one is genius. Though it begs more questions. Let's start with, "Am I losing my mind?" and move swiftly on to, "Did they see me coming?"

Somebody once told me that owning a gym is a good line of business, because 80 percent of the people who pay for the facility never turn up and actually use it. You can oversell your capacity and never worry about it. It's free money. The twenty-five-year guarantee on a casket strikes me as the same thing.

This particular casket looks like the starship *Enterprise*, and while it comes without the dodgy dialects and funny-shaped ears, it does come with a far-reaching price tag of eighteen thousand dollars plus tax.

The casket is way too lavish for my liking, certainly not the kind of vessel I can ever see myself being buried in. It's big and gold and sparkly. In fact, is that . . . yes, it looks like glitter. My daughter has a penchant for making boxes covered in glitter. I don't want to sound like I don't love my daughter or her craft activities, she is after all only five years old, but glittery boxes are generally bloody ugly. But one thing I must concede: I have met the kind of people who might purchase such a casket faux pas. I can hear one of his colleagues reading the epitaph:

In life he was a pretentious,
overbearing, attention-seeking ass.
In death he remains a pretentious,
overbearing, attention-seeking ass.

It seems to me that the dead were, at least in times of yore, respected and slightly feared. As a child I always saw the dead as being surrounded by light footsteps and careful whispers. We know too well that death is coming for us and can, if it so chooses, come out of the blue, when we are far from ready, and so we handle death, at least we did, with care. We paid Death his due respect and tried to stay on his good side. If we laughed or sneered at his victims we did it from a distance, in private. But in this new era of death-as-entertainment, it seems to me that one of Death's key functions is to make a mockery of the bereaved. Not through the death itself of a loved one, but through the checkout line that the bereaved have to pass through. I mean really, how does someone selling a casket with a twenty-five-year guarantee keep a straight face? And pushing the twenty-five-year con to one side for a minute, what is the purpose of an eighteen-thousand-dollar deluxe burial home? Gary Lee Ober was nearly skeletonized after a month. Imagine two months, or even three. Do you really care at that point if there are bugs in your box? The eighteen-thousand-dollar deluxe burial home is probably supplying lavish living quarters for the very bugs you are trying to avoid. So why would you put somebody in such a thing only to bury it deep underground? Are you going to take photos and show them at tea parties? Probably not. Is it a question of peace of mind?

Is it guilt? Does mere handing over of large sums of cash at the "death stall" make up for all the times you let your dear departed down?

I am told that people don't want to be seen as cheap in the face of death. Is that so? Well, I do! I want a flat-edged, austere, red oak box. I will arrange it all beforehand if that's what I need to do to ensure that I am not sent into the ground in some oversized, shiny, copper-coated monster. In fact, I will deal with it right now.

NOTE TO NEXT OF KIN

Apologies for the air of morbidity, but I have a few things I would like to clear up. Should death strike me unwittingly anytime in the near, or distant, future, I would like you to adhere to my few simple requests:

Put me to the flame immediately. Waste no time. Get me straight in there. I do not want to be put on display, with the upper half of my rigor-mortis-stiffened body poking out so that people can come and weep at the sight of me lying there . . . *dead*. I do not want to be groomed, made up, or hairstyled. My container should be of plain wood; if it could be something along the lines of my current living room cabinet, that would be most agreeable. In fact, if said cabinet is indeed still around, fold me over and put me in there. My ashes are then to be buried in Copenhagen, where I imagine my children and grandchildren to be living. I do not want my ashes in an urn; please just place them, containerless, into the ground. I would like a plain concrete headstone, one foot by one foot. On this I would like the words *Alan Emmins 1974–XXXX* and not one syllable more. For this task I appoint you the handsome budget of two thousand Great American Dollars.

You should consider this a legal document.
Yours,
Alan Emmins

My requirements have nothing to do with being cheap. I just don't want the hoo-ha. I want to take up as little space as possible with a marker so that my children or grandchildren know where to place the occasional bunch of lilies. The rest of the money that would normally be spent on a funeral I would recommend being spent on some kind of celebration, involving lashings of champagne and many toasts proclaiming what a splendid guy I was.

But luckily for Graham, who stands here with me now in the showroom of the Halsted N. Gray Funeral Home, the average person doesn't want what I want. They want eighteen-thousand-dollar carnival floats and two days of mourning services in the chapel. They want hair and makeup, a nice suit, and some gentle background music. They want twenty-five-year guarantees.

"This here is the rental casket," Graham tells me with a wave of his arm as he nods toward a highly polished, decorative, and open-topped ballroom of a casket. "This is used when people want a cremation, but they want to display the body for a memorial service beforehand. They can rent this casket for that purpose. If families want an immediate cremation with no service, this is the minimum container required."

The minimum container is an unornamented oblong of

chipboard. There are no shiny handles or guarantees. *Game on!* Now we're getting somewhere. Although, back up if you will. It may be minimal in all ways, and hacked together from no more than two floorboards, but it still costs $545. How can this be?

I feel a little disgusted by the prices. It seems a bit shameful. Why should these things cost so much? I can't help but think that the funeral industry is preying a little on the bereaved. I'll even concede to the twenty-five-year guarantee, but why can the caskets not just focus on function as opposed to being so very caught up on form? Then they would cost a quarter of the price.

Still, they don't cost a quarter of the price, and those shocking numbers lead me to feel that people are being duped. Regardless of their wealth and station while alive, they are being sold opulence when dead.

Sure, we have moved on over the years. People are no longer buried with their pets for company. Superstition has been pushed aside for things more tangible. The personal items of the dead have been replaced by items with price tags. Items that belong to a billion-dollar industry.

"How does the average person go about choosing a casket?" I ask Graham as he walks me around.

"A lot of it is eye appeal. We have many different types of wood. We have mahoganies—a lot of families find the wood to be warmer."

Graham is what you might expect in a funeral director. He is tall and slim and immaculately dressed. I doubt that even Neal could find a speck of dust on this guy. His manner is slow and calculated. His speech is soft, as if I myself have recently died and he's about to break it to me.

"But it's such a bizarre thing to me," I whisper to Graham as I look around the fifty-casket showroom. "The caskets are just so extravagant, considering what they're used for and where they're going to go. I mean, it's just . . . They just have so much decorative—"

"Some do, yes," he interrupts. "But like this one, for example, it doesn't at all," says Graham, pointing to a wooden casket next to him. "This is actually very plain. It's beautiful, it's mahogany. It's like a piece of furniture."

"Yeah, okay," I say.

I consent. The wood is beautiful. It *is* like a piece of furniture, but that's the part that I just don't get. Do I need to bring attention to the fact that it is not a piece of furniture, it's a casket! It will not be dined upon or used to display the best china. It's a box that's going in the ground with someone inside rotting like a bowl of fruit left in the sun for three months.

"We have copper and bronze . . ." says Graham, moving on. "Solid copper here."

Most of the caskets are the kind that have a split top so that the upper half can be left open for display. Most really could be put to better use floating down an avenue with Miss Funeral Home 2009 perched on the top, waving to the crowds on either side of the street. I guess I'm just a bit blown away by this room. I can't imagine how somebody in the midst of grieving feels when confronted by such a sight, or by such prices. Does it help them grieve to have to focus on so much choice; does it take their minds off their recent loss? Or does it just seem a bit ridiculous?

"What about this guarantee?" I ask Graham as we pass another gilded envelope with a number 25 on it. "It's a pretty safe guarantee to offer when you consider the dead are unlikely to bring any faults to the attention of the manufacturer?"

"Yeaaah," Graham says, and to my absolute delight he says it somewhat reluctantly.

As we leave the casket showroom we pass through a small room where the urns are on display. The sight of them confirms that I do not wish to have one. They range in price from $300 to about $1200. There is a nice star-spangled cookie tin for just $575.

"Do many people go for that star-spangled thing?"

"Well, we've only just brought that in, so . . ."

Graham takes me up a wide, carpeted stairway where he continues showing me the facilities. It's a big, big place. Like a grand old house. Along with the offices, the embalming facilities are upstairs. They seem so sterile with the tiled walls and halogen lights. By contrast, the four in-house chapels on the ground floor, which vary in splendor and decor according to available budget, are all about coziness. There are dried flower arrangements and candles, chairs set out in neat rows, and low, gentle music in the background. The carpets are dark and so thick that they muffle sound. When I see somebody approaching Graham and me with a walk that offers very little movement above the waist, and with a somber look on her face, who has actually gone to great efforts to look like a banshee with her long wiry hair, I realize that I have it all wrong: the funeral business is, in fact, not without humor.

It's also not without profit. Business-information site ibisworld.com reports that the funeral home industry turned over some $16.6 billion in 2005.

It seems one noise the dead can make is, "Cha-*ching!*"

And that is fine. There are plenty of people out there to help with the transaction. Like Neal, who did once consider becoming a mortician and who should maybe add this option to his current service. At the minimum he could start offering caskets, maybe even sell them from the back of his truck.

CRIME SCENE CASKETS: TAILORED TO FIT WHATEVER'S LEFT.

Why do people have to stop dying when I'm in town? How many days do I have to go without a suicide? Without a murder? Every day I wake up and am annoyed that I am not already awake: that I wasn't woken up at three in the morning because fifteen people were mowed down with a submachine gun in a McDonald's. I am panicking. I call Neal every two hours to see what's going on. Naturally, he is getting annoyed with my constant haranguing. But with every passing day, hour, and minute I get more irritated that people aren't killing themselves. Whenever my phone does ring I stare at it wide-eyed, mouthing the words, *Please be dead! Please be dead! Please be dead!* But, alas, they are, invariably, alive.

This morning, leaving Starbucks, I let the door slam in somebody's face. I didn't even react, I just moved on. Three days ago I would have leaped out of my seat at such insolence. Today I find myself simply disappointed that the glass in the door didn't shatter and slice the vital arteries of the woman who stood there staring at me in consternation. Did she not know that I have a book to write? That I can't write about dead people if they are still alive? And if I'm honest with myself, that's what all my panic and fear comes down to: this is my first commissioned book and I need people to die in order to complete it. I came here with the intention of highlighting how people use death and I have in the process become all the things that I despised before landing.

My phone rings.

"Hey, it's me," my ex-wife says through the phone.

"Hey, how are you? How's the worm?"

"We're good. You don't sound too happy, though. Is everything okay?"

"No, it's a nightmare. Nobody has died for eight days. I've flown and driven all this way and all I'm doing is watching fucking movies and drinking coffee. It's costing money to be here and—"

"Yeah, but, Alan, *come on*!"

"I know all about 'come on,' Christine, but what am I going to do if nobody dies? I have nothing to write about. How am I supposed to finish this book if—"

"But do you really feel comfortable complaining about that?"

"What does comfort have to do with it?"

"I thought you wanted to highlight that attitude as a bad thing," she reminds me. "Do something else. I can understand you're frustrated if all you're doing is watching movies every day. Do some research or something."

"I know, I know. . . . And I am, too. Tonight I am going to a bereavement-counseling session."

"Well, that could be a good interview, no?" Christine asks encouragingly.

"I'm not interviewing anybody. As a rule they don't let journalists in. So I called up and told them that my dad had died. I'm going to sit in on a group session to—"

"Alan, for God's sake!" Christine gasps in horror. "What are you thinking of?"

Sadly, I don't really know. Half of me is shocked by my behavior, knotted with compunction; the other half of me is on my knees, hands together and looking at the sky. I have started to feel out of my depth. Not just with the task of writing a book about death, but at finding myself confronted by my own shallowness. Taken away from my friends and family, I have no compass to guide me. I don't understand how I got so lost. I certainly hadn't been expecting it. Is it just because I've been surrounded by death? Is it watching people crawl out of the woodwork to sell off the possessions of relatives who decomposed on the sofa for a month? Is it the con of twenty-five-year guarantees? Suicide? Murder? Putty knives? Songs about scabby knees and hanging heads?

I think at this point Christine's phone call has just saved me from crossing a terrible line. Misrepresenting myself to people suffering the most terrible loss and grief would be an outrageous leap.

I take the piece of paper with the phone number and address for tonight's counseling session and I tear it up. I place it in a trash can on the sidewalk.

"Why don't you give Rachel a call," Christine suggests. "Go out for dinner again?"

She is right. My dependence on death is eating away at

my character. I do need a change. When we finish talking, I take Christine's advice and call Rachel.

"Walnut Creek? You're still in Walnut Creek?" Rachel asks, incredulous.

"Waiting for people to die, believe it or not," I say, thinking that I heard another question and lacking the enthusiasm to correct myself when the real question sinks in.

"Oh, that sucks. Hey, listen, I have an idea. One of my roommates has suddenly moved out. There's an empty room here now. Why don't you come and stay here for a few days?"

"Would that be okay?" I ask hopefully. "I really do need a change."

"Sure, but I'm not around tonight. But you can just come over and we'll grab a coffee and I'll give you some keys."

I am packing my case as if I am late for the airport. The relief I feel is instant and it washes over me in a tide of joy. Good-bye motel, depressing little hovel that you are. I examine the room and the bathroom, looking for forgotten items. It's a gloomy place. It's not surprising that many of the suicides Neal cleans up are in motel rooms. Renting a room does, after all, show a certain seriousness about what you're contemplating. If you choose a motel as your exit point, you have put thought into several important aspects of your suicide. The biggest being that you are unlikely to be disturbed while attaching yourself to the ceiling fan with the TV cord. You are unlikely to be interupted by your wife coming home early, or your roommate entering your room to see if you have any clean socks. You will not see a framed picture of your children, or a pair of shoes that remind you of the good times that might still be possible.

You will also, by using motel facilities, be ensuring that a loved one won't be confronted by your dead body, possibly swinging from the aforementioned ceiling fan, or casually lounging on the bed with a Jackson Pollock homage where your head used to be. You are ensuring that your loved one, friend, or fellow student will not have to get down on his or her hands and knees to clean up your scattered remains. You are sparing these people tainted furnishings and a room condemned to bad memories. If you check into a motel room intent on ending your life, you may consider yourself serious about it. Good-bye.

I, luckily, am serious only about bidding farewell to this motel.

Everybody in the house, including Rachel, welcomes me unquestioningly. They offer me beer and invite me to play games of pool. They invite me to theaters and bars that they are already attending with other friends. I go for Mexican food with one of Rachel's roommates, Cat, on her motorcycle. It's a warm evening, and I can think of nothing better to do than zap around San Francisco while clinging to the back of a motorcycle.

"You can ride back if you like," says Cat, as we leave the restaurant and find ourselves in front of her motorcycle.

"Are you kidding?" I ask, shocked at the offer. I *can* ride a motorcycle, but Cat has no way of knowing this.

But I don't take Cat up on her offer. I don't want to head home yet. If I go home now I am going to sit around thinking about death. I will sit half watching television, half watching my cell phone. I really feel like I need to make an effort to free my mind of the morbid, even if only for an evening.

After all, I haven't thought, or discussed, anything except death since I left L.A.

"I have a tropical farm about ten miles away; you should come and see it."

Yes, this really is the opening line of a conversation, and even though I do want to talk about things other than death, this isn't exactly what I had in mind.

I am in sitting on a stool at a bar. The guy sitting next to me, also alone, is around sixty years old, clearly a madman and drunk to boot.

"Wonderful though the offer may be—" I start to tell the guy, but he cuts me off halfway through.

"Let me buy you a drink," he says.

"No, that's okay. I'll get my own." To the barman I say, "A Corona, please."

But as the barman places my drink on the bar, the guy next to me says. "Here, George, it's on me."

"No, really, I'd rather buy my own," I insist, looking at the barman.

But the barman ignores my hand, which is holding out money, and removes a ten-dollar bill from the little pile of money Mr. Tropical has sitting on the bar.

I get that it is rude to refuse a drink, but surely it is down to me whether I want to be rude or not? I can't help thinking that the dead, and the people who deal with them, are a lot less complicated than the average Joe. But stop! I am back on the subject of death again. Shake that thought. Regroup.

"I have a tropical farm about ten miles away; you should

come and see it," the man next to me repeats, leaning toward me this time.

"Are you mad?"

"What do you mean—*mad*?"

"You've already invited me to your tropical farm once."

"And?"

"And I said *no*."

"We can chase after the ostriches!"

At this point he slips off his stool and I have to catch him.
I drink up, thank the old guy for the beer, and leave as quickly
as I can. He is still talking to me as I walk out through the
door and turn the corner.

A few blocks down, I come across a used bookstore
that's open until ten thirty. *That will do,* I think to myself. I
spend a lot of time in bookshops, so this should help me get
back on familiar ground.

Late-night book shopping is actually something I miss
from my days living in New York City. There's something
great about buying books in the evening. Because you have
the time to browse and read a few pages of every book you
pick up, you often leave with books that you weren't looking for.

An hour later, I leave with *Old Goriot,* by Balzac, and
walk back to an Italian café that I passed on the way down.
There is only one table available outside. It's big and has five
chairs around it, but the waitress says it's okay to take it while
I wait for a smaller table. As soon as my glass of wine arrives,
a party of four turns up and wants the table. They sit down
with me. There's a mother, father, son, and the son's friend.
The boys are around thirteen years old.

"Hi, I'm Isaac. I'm a writer," the friend informs me.

"Fantastic," I say, choking a little on my wine.

This is a pretty typical Disney family. Good-looking, successful-looking, confident, and out enjoying themselves. The mother is tall with blond hair, little makeup, and incredible cheekbones. The father looks like a businessman. He has a warm smile and an air of confidence. When he and his wife catch each other's eyes there's a sparkle. The son seems like a nice guy.

But then there's this Isaac character. Absolutely too good-looking for his age and totally aware of it; *the little bastard.* He has too much hair, to start with. Hair that seems to flip and flop like he's in a shampoo commercial (which he probably is), and on top of all that he has way too much confidence.

"What do you do?" he inquires while holding my eye.

"Me?" I pause "I write . . ." and then, realizing how silly this now sounds and wanting to get out of it, I say, "birthday cards."

"You do? Oh my God! *And you tell people?* Brad, did you hear that? He writes birthday cards. I didn't think people really did that."

"That's so funny!" Brad says.

"I write poetry, mainly," says Isaac. "And novels."

"Interesting," I say back, finding myself wanting to punch Isaac in the face.

"Where are you from?" the mother asks.

"England," I say.

"We're all San Francisconites," says Isaac, cutting the conversation off.

I smile at the mother, who actually looks back at me with a smile that says *I know,* and then winks at me. I am unsure whether this is to confirm that they are all indeed San Francisconites or to confirm that Isaac is indeed a little pubescent twat worthy of a punch on the nose.

I slowly raise *Old Goriot* and slouch down in my chair. But there's a part of me that is looking at this little happy group and wondering if they have any idea how vulnerable their lives are. What happens to such strong units when death strikes? How do they cope? How do they move on? There's nothing to stop them from having a tragic car crash on the way home. Or to enter their front door to be confronted with a gun-wielding and slightly panicked burglar.

"Balzac," I hear Isaac ponder. "Balzac," he whispers again.

Is he talking to me? I wonder. Can he tell that I came out to get away from death but in fact, once again, was spiraling off with macabre thoughts about his own mortality? Isaac's pretensions make me focus all my thoughts on him and the fact that were he to meet his unwitting, bloody end this evening, based on his location, there's a very good chance that his remains would be introduced to Neal Smither.

A couple at another table gets up to leave. I quickly grab my wine and leave this poet to his Diet Coke.

The evening is perfect for sitting outside with a book and a glass of wine. But that doesn't mean that I am going to sit and read. Oh no. I am truly back on death now and sit watching strangers pass me by, calculating the odds of their one day meeting Neal Smither.

Take the girl whose dog just considered pissing up my leg. Here she is asking me about the book I am pretending to read, but all I can think about, as she stands there smiling, is that if she is murdered tonight, in a messy manner that no relative wanted to clean up, there has to be a 60 percent chance that Neal would get the job. Eighty percent if she is murdered in a public space.

Neal does pretty good business across America, but this is his home turf. He has the advantage here.

The people on the street have no clue just how good the odds of their meeting Neal really are. Because, let's face it, unless they die in a hospital, or in their sleep and are discovered within seventy-two hours, the odds in favor of a Neal-shaped encounter are pretty damn good.

I drink to that and order another glass of wine.

The room that I am staying in is large and bare with polished wooden floors. In the middle of this floor is a single-width futon. That's where I lie. Rubbing my eyes and trying to gauge the severity of my hangover. My suitcase is in the corner. I look at the alarm clock: 9:15. It's the first time I've slept past seven since I arrived in the United States.

I really like this room and can't help but fantasize about moving in. I would keep it the way it is, bare, nothing but the futon and my suitcase. It occurs to me that if I were ever to commit suicide, I'd like it to be in a room like this. Bare, empty, and with nicely worn wooden floors. Which in itself marks another change in my way of thinking. I have never before sat pondering preferred methods and locations for my pending death.

I decide to phone Neal, with a desire to get back to concentrating on other people's deaths.

"Nah, sorry, dude, nothing happening, but don't go getting depressed, Alan. I'll get you on the phone the second something happens. There's nothing you can do when this happens, Alan, except . . . ?"

"Pray for death?"

"You got it," Neal says as he hangs up.

CRANK HOUSE

The following morning my phone rings. "Alan, I got a crank house for you," says Neal as a form of greeting. "Meet me there. Here's the address."

Slowly but surely I am becoming familiar with the area. For example, I no longer use my map to find the interstate that I need. But that's where the familiarity stops: with directions. My grasp of American terminology, while improving, is still lacking. For example, I am on my way to a "crank house," although I don't really know what a crank house is. I do know that the job is for one of Neal's national motel contracts; so is *crank* slang for something related to the motel industry? Or is it simply Neal terminology for a scumbag? It could easily be.

Neal is already on the scene when I arrive, his truck taking up two parking spaces in the car lot. The motel is fairly typical. A single oblong block holding rooms on two floors. I guess there are about twenty rooms to a floor, double that if there are rooms at the back of the building, too. As I pull up outside I am taken with the fact, possibly for the first time, that I really like the look of motels, even if they are a bit ratty. There's something about all those strangely colored doors in a long row like that, like soldiers clad in full regalia standing at attention, that just appeals to me. Motels are like a throwback from European images of 1950s America. Remove the cars from the lot and it could be any year. Remove the DO NOT CROSS tape, the two fire engines, the ambulance, the police cars, and the crowd of astonished, evacuated guests, and this place would be an ideal image of the America I loved as a kid.

"Why would you do that?" I hear an officer asking me, even though all the windows of my car are up. "You can see the bright yellow tape, right? So why pull in here?"

"I'm with Crime Scene Cleaners," I tell him.

"Where's your truck?"

"I don't have one."

The officer doesn't reply to me, but radios up to a colleague. ". . . Yeah, you got the Crime Scene Cleaner guy up there? . . . Is he expecting—" He stops and looks at me and asks, "What's your name?"

"Alan," I tell him, trying to be as polite and unobjectionable as I can.

"Ask him if he is expecting anybody, and if so, what's the name."

A few seconds pass. If Neal is not actually right there, I realize, I am going to be sent away. But luckily my name comes over the radio and the officer holds the tape up so I can drive under.

"Tell him to get you a truck," he says with a smile as I drive past.

As I pull up to the parking bay, I watch several officers who are hanging around outside a room on the second floor that has been taped off; they are holding their hands over their noses. So a crank house is a room where a body has decomposed?

Climbing the stairs to the upper level, passing suspicious officers as I go, my nostrils are filled with a strong odor of cat urine. A crank house must be a room filled with cat waste? Is that why the firemen are coming and going with their masks on?

I enter the room on which all attention is focused. I can hear somebody asking me if my name is Alan, but I am finding it hard not to stare at the television that is sitting on the floor. MTV is playing 50 Cent. A collective of beautiful black girls appears to be rubbing themselves against him. 50 Cent stands there, as would I, grinning like a wanton fool. A TV depicting gyrating black beauties was just about the last thing I was expecting to see on entering this room. I drag my eyes from the screen and my attention is caught by something else. The table in front of me is covered with what look like burn marks; it has even melted in places. On the table are some spoons, some rubber tubes, a couple of Pyrex dishes, and several jars that are blackened or yellowed or in some cases both. Coffee filters lie everywhere, both on the table and on the floor. Some of them are unused. Others are stained red. Likewise, matchboxes are scattered all about the room, open and with their redheaded children sprinkled all around the room. The strike pads on the sides of the boxes appear to have been scraped off. Also scattered around the room are empty packets of Sudafed—*lots* of empty packets of Sudafed. The cardboard boxes litter one half of the room, while the now empty foil packets from inside sit mainly around the floor under the table.

On the bed is an empty box that once held breathing masks. Next to that there's another box, also empty, that was once full of surgical gloves. Several large white bottles with hardware-store labels indicating muriatic acid are lined against the bottom of a wall. Next to those are some empty Prestone antifreeze containers.

I finally understand: a crank house is a makeshift chemical-weapons factory!

In another corner there is a large cardboard box that says it held glass jars. There's a smashed blender by the door and a gasoline can in the sink. Above some drawers are three sets of twin hotplates. In the bathroom, actually in the bath, there's a small gas cylinder.

Of course, it's not a chemical-weapons factory. If it were, I wouldn't be in here. Neither would Neal, unless this morning he changed the writing on his truck to read HOMICIDES, SUICIDES, ACCIDENTAL DEATHS and CHEMICAL WEAPONS LABORATORIES. But in another sense it is a chemical-weapons factory. America is the biggest producer of this particular kind of home-grade chemical weapon, and the Americans who produce it, for the most part, use the chemical on themselves. A crank house, then, is a methamphetamine laboratory.

Crystal meth has a reputation as a one-hit addiction drug: stronger than coke and heroin combined. Meth addiction has spread from state to state like bushfire. In the last decade, meth-lab reports have dotted the map of the USA like a Hollywood doomsday scenario. At its worst peak, 1,287 clandestine, or "mom and pop" lab incidents were dealt with by the authorities in California alone. Across the United States this rose to a total of 17,356 lab incidents.

Of those who choose to dabble in the precarious art of meth production, the lucky ones will probably find themselves closed up in dark solitude, covered in scars, scabs, and open sores, and will most definitely be missing several teeth from their rotted gums. The unlucky ones, like Amber McNeally from Iowa, whom I interviewed for an article about meth, find themselves severely burned.

Meth's success is linked largely to its easy production, especially in Middle America, where most ranches use anhydrous ammonia to maximize the fertilization of their ground. Anhydrous ammonia is a key ingredient in meth production, and meth cooks can simply walk up to the big white anhydrous tanks that dot most ranches and siphon off as much as they need. For those willing to risk the wrath of farmer Brown, it's free; it's literally on tap. It's therefore no wonder that twelve- to fourteen-year-olds who live in small towns are more than twice as likely to use meth than those who live in large cities.

After anhydrous ammonia, there are only four items left on the meth production shopping list: lithium batteries, ethanol, coffee filters, and ephedrine.

Ephedrine, or pseudoephedrine, sounds like it might be something scarce, hard to get hold of, but it is actually the main ingredient of common cold tablets available in all drugstores and supermarkets across America.

Once your shopping list is complete, all you need is forty-five minutes of your time, a wooden spoon, and an Internet connection to download a three-step instruction manual. The easiest and most popular process for cooking meth is known as the "Nazi Method." Supposedly, it is the same method used by the Germans in World War II, who produced meth and fed it to their troops to keep them going. The Germans weren't the only ones fueling their troops with meth: the English and the Americans soldiers often were on it too; as were Japan's kamikaze pilots.

During the first half of this decade, while the problem remained for the most part in Middle America, meth wasn't of much concern to the U.S. government. But then one day it hopped over the Mississippi River and marched straight into Washington. By the time the capital woke up to meth, it had already consumed most of the U.S. drug market, and at one hundred dollars a gram it is now outselling long-standing favorites such as coke and heroin.

Without pseudoephedrine there would be no meth, but the pharmaceutical companies will not stop producing pseudoephedrine—nor will the government make them—because cold pills are a billion-dollar-a-year industry.

Of course, the government and pharmaceutical companies would never openly support meth abuse, but many states have more licensed drugstores than their population can sustain, and these drugstores all get their pseudoephedrine pills legally. They sell them legally, too: in any quantity and to anybody who walks through their doors.

It isn't just the ease of production or the simple ingredients that make meth the drug of choice. It is also the fact that meth can be produced pretty much anywhere. Motel rooms, as Neal will testify, have long been popular lab converts: you can check in, turn the room into a highly explosive and poisonous location, and check out again without concerning yourself about who's going to do the chores. In fact, across most of the United States you can rest assured that Crime Scene Cleaners will deal with the situation for you. Neal makes a point of selling the service and now includes it on his Web site and in his brochures.

Meth is also a logistically convenient drug. With heroin or cocaine you need to wait for plant growth, but meth can be produced quickly and cheaply, within U.S. borders. You don't lose men or money trying to smuggle large consignments across borders; you don't even need to deal in large consignments. Just produce what you need when you need it. You could produce a week's supply on one day and be selling it in the school playground the next.

The meth situation has gotten so bad in the United States that it simply can't be ignored. Drug task forces have been set up especially to tackle this problem. Today, meth-lab seizures are down, and not because they are harder to find, but because the ingredients are harder to get. In many states, farmer Brown has had to lock his anhydrous tanks, and in many others there are now limits on how many cold pills you are allowed to buy over-the-counter. This may sound like a win, but it has brought with it other problems. Removing meth from the streets did not remove the well-established dependency. So production went down but the consumer demand didn't. Now the drug *is* being smuggled in. Meth production has been taken out of the hands of the small dealers and users and put into the hands of the bigger crime syndicates.

Still, when meth labs are found, and they are (5,080 in the United States in 2007, of which 221 were in California), there's a lot of caution. The chemicals produced by, or used in, meth production are highly lethal, and not only as poisons— hydrogen, for example, is highly flammable and lighter than air. Reports in the U.S. media of exploding meth houses are not hard to find. Needless to say, when I find him in the motel room, Neal is not his usual, jovial self.

"Alan—there's acid and all kinds of shit in these jars," he says through his breathing mask as he approaches. "I can't be responsible for you. You gotta wait outside, and I don't mean outside the door. Go get yourself a coffee. I'll call you when I'm done."

I realize it would be a dim-witted assumption to consider all the containers and jars in this room to be empty. A gallon of ether holds the same explosive power as six sticks of dynamite. I don't argue with Neal. I tell him to be safe, and I get the hell out of Dodge.

MAN IN THE BATH PART III: THE STATE *VS* JAMES MCKINNON

The San Francisco Superior Court is pure entertainment. Every walk of life is represented here, from the continual offender who appears to know the building like the back of his hand to teenagers who look scared out of their minds over a traffic offense. The corridors are lined with lawyers holding armfuls of files, police officers waiting to give evidence, reporters looking for a scoop, and cameramen covering high-profile cases. They stand around, bored, but poised in case the door to *their* courtroom opens. They fill the hours of waiting with banter.

"I'm not even supposed to be here," a sketch artist tells a camera crew sitting on a bench outside a trial. She is shading a sketch of a man in a suit who sits in the witness stand. "I should be preparing for the Scott Peterson trial."

"Preparing?" asks the cameraman with excessive interest, looking from friend to friend to get their attention "What do you have to do to prepare, sharpen your pencils?"

The corridor fills with the kind of laughter that says: "You're not one of us."

The floors are polished and the doors are wood paneled. The courtrooms are spread out in rows on several floors, with jury lists and case numbers pinned to the doors. There's a real pulse of life, like one of those nature films where they show the speeded-up growth of a flower. One minute, the corridors quiet down, with only a few people scattered on benches. Then a courtroom opens its doors and crowds of people swarm out, digging in their pockets for cigarettes or striding fast toward the toilets. Conversation becomes animated.

"But what about when he said—"

"The next witness is the one—"

"The judge doesn't like him—"

I enjoy listening to the banter as I sit waiting. For my part, I am here to meet a court clerk: I have ordered a copy of the transcript for the preliminary trial of Jim McKinnon and am here to collect. As soon as I have the paper-packed manila envelope in my hand, I rush back out into the corridor, fling myself onto a bench, and start reading.

Gary Lee Ober lived in his studio apartment at 182 Bemis Street, in San Francisco, for around fifteen years. Throughout this time he developed a long-term friendship with his neighbor, Stephanie Henry.

"His apartment was directly opposite mine; we used to leave our front doors open and pretend that we had a mansion."

As Stephanie told Assistant District Attorney Elliot

Beckelman early on in the preliminary trial, the problems started when Stephanie knocked on Ober's door one day with some bad news.

"I had a Pomeranian named Aiza, and Lee loved my dog, we all loved him. He was a person to us.

"I went to Lee's apartment on one particular day and knocked at the door. I asked for Lee, to tell him that my Pomeranian had been killed. My exact words to Mr. Mc-Kinnon were, 'Tell him that someone very dear to us has died.' "

At the time in question, Gary Lee Ober would have been just on the other side of the door, decomposing in a bathtub. I would imagine that this announcement, that "someone very dear to us has died," would have sent a chill of panic down McKinnon's spine. But no: McKinnon had obviously put thought into this inevitable encounter. His yarn was already spun. He told Stephanie that *his* friend Gary Lee Ober was away on a seven-thousand-dollar Disney cruise that he had won. Apparently, he wouldn't be back for two weeks.

"I was very shocked," Stephanie told the court. "I even said to Mr. McKinnon, 'Wow, he didn't tell me anything about it.' Lee was positively boastful, you know. He would have told me if he went on a cruise. I told him, 'Usually, he gives me a set of keys.' "

Jim McKinnon aroused further suspicions as his encounter with Stephanie Henry went on. She asked McKinnon to have Ober call her when he next checked in.

Two weeks later, when there was still no sign of Ober, Stephanie crossed the hall to confront McKinnon again about the whereabouts of her friend.

"I said [to McKinnon], 'Where's Lee?' You know. 'You told me it would be this day,' and it wasn't. He said, 'Oh I forgot. I made a mistake. It's not this week. It's going to be the week after next.'"

"So two weeks later, when you had that conversation with Mr. McKinnon concerning the whereabouts of your friend, Lee," began the assistant DA, "did you notice something about the apartment unit itself? Any odors or any sights that caused you concern?"

"Yes."

"And what were those odors or concerns?"

"The odor, the odor, the odor," repeated Stephanie.

"How would you describe that?"

"Very pungent, very strong. But I thought it was something in the back, outside, because we live in quite a woodsy area."

"I see," continued the assistant DA. "And besides an odor, did you observe anything else in the complex that caused you concern?

"Yes."

"What was that?"

"The flies."

Stephanie and another neighbor went out and bought cans of Black Flag fly spray. They began attacking the flies, but the chemical warfare had little effect on the numbers they were dealing with. No matter how much they sprayed, the walls in the hallway were still covered with thousands of flies. Just recalling this in the witness stand brought Stephanie to tears, and the judge called for a recess.

"I was supposed to go to work that day that I did call the

police, but I was throwing up," Stephanie continued when the court resumed. "I was nauseous to my stomach, and I was irritated because no one could smell what I smelled.

"And I don't know, maybe because it was just he and I on the top level, but it was so strong and I was throwing up. I was literally in my bathroom. My mom was there. I was throwing up. She was very concerned, and I just said, 'Something's not right. I don't feel right. My gut feeling is telling me something's not right,' because I did speak to him again . . ."

"Jim McKinnon?" inquired the assistant DA.

"Yes."

"Yes?"

"And I said to him when I last spoke to him, 'You told me that Lee was going to be here,' and I kind of got irritated. I said, 'Now it's been a long time.'"

"I'm assuming—and you tell me if I'm wrong—that you had again gone to Lee Ober's apartment and knocked on the door. Is that correct?"

"Yes."

"And the conversation you had with Mr. McKinnon. Mr. McKinnon was inside the apartment?"

"Yes."

"And he opened the door partially?"

"He cracked it open, just cracked it open. If you want to say that this is five inches, and then large enough just for him to stick his head out."

"And how soon after that did you call the police?"

"Mr. McKinnon was gone the next day."

"Is that when you called the police?" the assistant DA asked.

"I want to say yes, that that was the next day. I don't want to quote and say for sure. Within the next day to two days I called the police."

I personally don't get this and have to stop reading for a minute. I lean back against the wall, wondering how this situation could have gone on for over a month. On paper it seems ridiculous. I mean, how many signs do you need before you pick up the telephone? A week? Sure, without the flies and the stench I could even wait out the two weeks that McKinnon had said Ober would be away on the cruise. When he didn't return after two weeks, then maybe a day or two more to notice, another couple if you are ill or busy at work. But all these signs coupled with the stench, the flies, and the stranger who won't open the door more than a few inches? Surely this creates enough suspicion for a phone call?

But this is coming from someone who once stepped over a man wearing a balaclava and clutching a gun, completely convinced that it was a joke, that somebody was after a cheap laugh at my expense. Because men with guns and balaclavas are things of TV, not everyday life. For most of us, our introduction to death comes from TV. Then we get it as a staple diet. It seems to me that our exposure to death-as-entertainment leads to a level of disbelief when confronted with real death, convincing us that we're only seeing fantasy.

Does the smell and those flies coming from my neighbor's apartment mean that he is dead? Or have I just been watching too much *Law & Order*? How blurred do the lines become when our own environment mirrors the horrors shown on any one drama on any one channel on any one night of the week? Are we becoming so exposed to this stuff that when it happens for real we just don't see it?

Crime scene investigator David Suyehiro was called to the stand to give the court a basic rundown of the state of the apartment as he entered 182 Bemis.

"Let's talk about the bathroom. Was there anything of significance in the bathroom?" asked the assistant DA.

"Right," began Inspector Suyehiro. "When you walked into the bathroom there was a lot of possible blood or staining. Inside the bathtub there was what appeared to be a decomposing body. As you walked straight into the bathroom, immediately to the right, there's a sink area. On top of the sink area there was a box of baking soda that was slightly spilled into the bowl of the sink. Also, as you walk further in, when you get to the bathtub area there looked like blood-staining on the shower curtain as well as on the tub, and inside the tub, as I said, there was a decomposing body. On the body there were some towels and also another box of baking soda."

"So it's your understanding that the gestation of an insect goes from a casing, to something that crawls out, to something that flies?" the assistant DA asked.

"Correct."

"In terms of casings, how many casings? Was it just a few casings, or do you have a generic way of saying roughly how many casings there were?"

"I would guess probably in the hundreds. There were quite a few."

"How about in terms of larvae? What is larvae, do you know?

"It's the stage of a fly's life where actually it kind of looks like a worm almost, slightly opaque in color, and they just basically crawl around."

"Did you find anything of significance in the hallway?" asked the assistant DA.

"As you walked into the hallway, once you passed the bathroom, there was a closet area. Inside this area there was a mop."

"What was significant about the mop?"

"The mop had a sponge head, and it had some staining on it."

"Was there any presumptive testing done on that staining?"

"Yes."

"And what were the presumptive-testing results?"

"Tested positive for blood."

"Would it be fair to say that the mop which had the presumptive test of blood was used . . . that one could conclude one was attempting to clean up blood?"

"Objection, Judge!" public defender Feldman called out at this point in the proceedings. "Speculation!"

"Sustained!" replied the Honorable Peter J. Busch.

The important substance of a court case is missing from the nightly TV dramas. Namely, that the proceedings are generally dull and go around in circles, discussing things that were established way back when the witness first took the stand. Lawyers stop, "May I have a moment, Judge . . . ?" so that they can flick through their papers, seemingly lost, possibly drifting in a maze of a dozen other cases. They are not playing for time, promoting a quietness that will let the last comment sink deep into the minds of those present. They are genuinely lost looking through their notes. They are not the sophisticated masters of rebuttal that they are depicted to be. The questioning meanders, and witnesses backtrack and change answers to questions that were posed ten minutes earlier.

"So when you're standing in the doorway of 182 Bemis, can you see into the bathroom?" public defender Feldman asked Stephanie Henry at one point.

"Not when the door's closed," she replied.

"So if you're going into the front door of 182 Bemis, the bathroom is on the left side?"

"Yes."

"Or is it on the right side?"

"Yes, it's on the left side."

"So when someone is in the doorway, you can't see into the doorway of the bathroom, right?"

"Right."

"And when you had that initial contact with Mr. McKinnon, he told you that Mr. Ober would be back the following Tuesday, is that right?"

"Correct."

"Just so that I have it clear in my mind, did you ever see Mr. McKinnon and Mr. Ober together?"

"Never."

"It's about at least a week from when you last saw Mr. Ober to when you first saw Mr. McKinnon, right, roughly?"

"Approximately."

"After August tenth, when did you see Mr. McKinnon again?"

The assistant DA cut in. "After the week of August the tenth?" he asked.

"Let me slow down," continued the public defender. "You have this conversation with Mr. McKinnon in the doorway of 182 Bemis around August the tenth. When is the next time you see—physically see—Mr. McKinnon?"

"When he was coming up the stairs and I was, too."

"How much after that initial meeting are we talking about?"

"Approximately four days, five days."

"Do you have a conversation with Mr. McKinnon at that time?"

"Yes."

"What do you talk about?"

"Him being drunk."

"So he's pretty drunk when he's coming home?"

"Yeah, and I laughed with him. I was kind of like, 'whoa,' you know, and he was like, he was pretty, pretty intoxicated."

"Pretty hammered?"

"Yeah."

"Do you watch Mr. McKinnon go into 182 Bemis, or do you go into your door before Mr. McKinnon goes into 182 Bemis?"

"Mr. McKinnon allowed me to go into my door first."

"What do you mean, he *allowed* you to go into your door first?"

"For whatever reason, he allowed me to go into my door first."

"Describe what you mean, please, ma'am."

"Just like when I first, when I just answered your question. As I remember, the bathroom door was open. It was not closed on the tenth: *it was open.*"

"So let me back you up. We're now going back to talk about August the tenth?"

Not only were they going back to talk about August the tenth, they were going back to talk about the bathroom door being open—a door that the witness stated couldn't even be seen when somebody was standing in the front doorway.

Dr. Stephens, San Francisco's medical examiner, was called to the stand.

"Dr. Stephens, are you familiar with the death of Gary Lee Ober?" inquired the assistant DA.

"Yes, sir, I am."

"Can you give your opinion about what the cause of death was concerning Gary Lee Ober?"

"The cause of death is sharp-force injury to the chest, counsel."

"Sharp force?" asked the judge.

"Sharp force," reiterated the medical examiner.

"What's that based on?" the assistant DA asked, taking up the questioning once again.

"It's based on the finding of two sharp-force injuries to cartilaginous portions of the rib cage. There was a portion between the bony rib and the breastbone, in older people it's filled with cartilaginous and calcified material. There were two sharp-force injuries within that material."

"Doctor, I'm handing you what's been marked as people's fifteen, sixteen, and seventeen. Those are three color photographs. Do you recognize fifteen?"

"I do recognize people's fifteen, sixteen, and seventeen, counsel."

"What is fifteen?"

"Fifteen is a photograph of the inside of the rib cage. The rib cage front portion has been taken off, and this view is looking from inside the chest towards the outside. It's marked on the photographs as to orientation. It shows the breastbone or sternum, as well as the adjacent portion of the ribs."

It occurs to me, as I sit here and read, that Dr. Stephens, like Neal, gets real up close and personal with the dead. The jobs have different functions, but there is no denying that they share a similar level of intimacy.

"Does fifteen show the two injuries that you previously made reference to?"

"Yes, sir, it does. There is a pair of instruments, one is pointing to each of the two injuries that are described."

"Can you tell whether or not . . . just to be clear, the injuries at the fourth and sixth rib, that's the location that led to the death of Gary Lee Ober?"

"That is our opinion, counsel. First of all, they are sharp-force injuries. They're in a particularly dangerous anatomic portion of the body. However, the body is badly decomposed and there's no clear indication of injuries to any structure or organs underneath."

"Based upon your training and experience, and this autopsy and the photographs that you have there, are you able to give an opinion about where the blood would be jettisoned or leaped to in this matter?"

"Not really. There's a considerable amount of material that's present in the bathroom where the body was found. Most of this is clearly decomposition fluid and some of it has been artifacted by another mechanism."

"What does that mean, 'artifacted'?"

"There's evidence that portions of the scene have been cleaned and, therefore, some of the decomposition fluids have been moved about, potentially contaminating parts of the scene.

"Probably the most significant thing is injuries like this are notorious for bleeding inside the body, so the actual scene of death may not be in the bathtub, and there may be little or no blood at the actual scene of death."

"I see. Doctor, are you able to give any sort of opinion about the window of time when this homicide occurred? Assuming that the body was discovered on September tenth . . . in the summertime, are you able to give a window of a period of time when Mr. Ober might have been killed?"

"Well, ordinarily to do an opinion of that nature we need to know when the person was last seen alive with certainty, and then, of course, when they were found, and then use the available information to give a basis of the most logical time of death based upon some information.

"In this particular case, flies have gone through a complete cycle from egg to the pupa and pupa have hatched. That's a temperature- and humidity-dependant factor for the common flies that can range from as little as seven to ten days, but in colder, dryer conditions it can be a month or more.

"I think, looking at the scene, we're probably talking about at least two weeks, maybe longer. The body was nearly skeletonized."

The benches in the corridors of the Superior Court building are not made for long reading sessions, and so with a numb backside I stuff the court transcript back into the manila envelope and head out for an early supper. Or at least I try. The doors to three courts open at once, and immediately the corridor fills with suits and squeaky shoes. With my silly English manners I am bounced around like a ball in a pin-ball machine as I make my way to the exit.

WHEN IT RAINS IT POURS

Alan, get in your car and drive to Campbell. You need to take 101 south towards San Jose, the 85 south towards Santa Cruz, then get on the 280 south, take the Hamilton Avenue exit, exit number 25; from there you need to find North First Street, number 70. You got it?"

"Neal, hold on, I need a pen."

"Alan, dude. Don't fuck around. If you want to make this job, you need to get going."

"Neal, I was asleep. I just need to get a pen. What time is it anyway?"

"It's two A.M."

"Okay, I've got a pen. So, 101 south, onto the 85, and then what?"

Even though Neal told me to hurry, I have to stop at the gas station for coffee. I need to wake up. Plus, I don't know how much I want to rush. I have had several days away from death now. I am recovering.

I enjoy driving through San Francisco in the early hours of the morning with a coffee in my hand. At two A.M. there is no traffic stopping and starting every ten feet. You can enjoy the characters on the street: the couple hugging and kissing in drunk abandon, the homeless guy singing songs to them for change, or maybe just singing songs, the officers sitting on the hood of their car drinking coffee. These are the things I want to see.

That said, I have a job to do.

When I arrive at 70 North First Street it is alive with police officers—so many that you would think a mass homicide had taken place. There's a huge cement truck pulled over to one side. People go back and forth, pointing at the ground. I can see Steve, one of the Crime Scene Cleaners, talking to a police officer. I park, slip on my Crime Scene Cleaners baseball cap as a means of ID, and head over.

There's an air of disbelief. People look shocked.

"Neal, this is crazy. It's off the fucking chart. You need to get out here," Steve is saying into his cell phone.

An elderly lady had stepped out into the road from between parked cars. Not only had the driver of the cement truck not seen her, he hadn't felt her as his truck hit her. It was only after, when his truck violently skidded for no apparent reason, that he stopped. He got out of the truck wondering what had happened.

He didn't find an old lady.

What he found were the pureed remains of one.

From the back of the truck, leading two hundred yards farther, is the smeared broken line of the old lady's remains, like the white line in the middle of the road, only red and matted with hair and fabric. It is a staggering mess. There's just so much blood. It's as if she were squeezed like a tube of toothpaste.

Neal arrives quickly, and after a swift appraisal of the scene gets on the phone and calls for two more guys to come help with the cleanup. He then signals to me.

"Dude, you've gotta come take a look at this."

I follow him over to where a group of officers stand around in amazement.

"See what that is?" Neal asks.

I stare down at the road and the red clump that sits there. It takes me a while to form words.

"It can't be, it just can't be," I say a little in awe.

"That's exactly what it is, my friend, her *heart*! Pretty fucking amazing, huh? Must a just popped right outta her when she was pressurized. That's pretty fucking amazing."

"Ever seen anything like that before?" one of the officers asks Neal.

"Like that? A fresh heart? Intact? Sitting in the middle of the road? Fuck no!"

In a sense, yes, it is pretty fucking amazing. The heart *is* intact. It is not squashed or torn. It doesn't lie in or with other remains. It is not in the middle of a puddle of blood. When the heart is removed by the medical examiner, it leaves behind a bloodstain that outlines its shape.

That will probably go on to be the saddest thing I have ever seen, I think to myself.

The reason why there are so many police on the street is because this accident happened right in front of the Campbell police station. The crime scene, if it is in fact a crime scene, has become a training camp, where the more experienced officers are taking on the role of teachers.

"So the first traces of blood are here," says one officer talking to a younger officer. "So she more than likely came out from between the parked cars somewhere about here, you see?"

It's not a difficult cleanup, but it is a lot of work. Douse each patch with enzyme, scrub with a stiff brush, and mop up with tissue. There are four Crime Scene Cleaners on the job and a neighbor who has made a tray of coffee. In all, the scrubbing and wiping takes around four hours. It's gory work. There's also no avoiding the fact that this is the old lady's hair and flesh that you are scrubbing. The fact that this was not a suicide but a bad accident makes it all the more poignant. You can only imagine the sweetest of grannies, even though in reality she may not have been. But the blood on the ground allows you only to imagine and your imagination wants to give you a little old lady wearing a cardigan and spectacles.

It's seven A.M. when all is done and people are starting to head home. I drive back along I 280, but decide not to go back into the city. The road is already jammed with people heading into San Francisco. I could easily spend the next two hours in traffic. I see a Motel 6 sign poking up into the sky and turn off.

I check in with a melancholy state of mind and slip into the motel bed, hoping that I can stop thinking about dead old ladies.

I awake with a start, unable to recall why I am in a motel room when I went to bed in Rachel's house in Twin Peaks. Then I remember.

"*Who* is it?" I'm asking the phone, confused.

"It's Shawn, Crime Scene Cleaners."

"Hey, Shawn, sorry. I was asleep. What's up?"

"Hey, I got one for you. Berkeley. Guy took his head off with a shotgun. You interested?"

"Yeah, I'm in a motel just off the 280. Where do I need to go?"

It's a mere two and a half hours since I checked in. The expression on the receptionist's face, as I check out so soon, tells me that my behavior is odd. But she also looks vaguely excited by something. Maybe I am a bank robber on the run. Maybe I escaped from prison and needed to rest before continuing my flight from the law. Maybe I'm a murderer. Oooooooooooooh.

I ask her where I can get coffee and she gives me directions to a McDonald's. While I am there I make a decision to eat, just in case I am on my way to a gruesome scene. I don't want the dry retches again. I don't want to be in pain for the next four days if I do get sick. And that's why I eat a large Quarter Pounder meal en route to a suicide.

The job is in a small storage room. Shawn tells me that somebody shot himself in the head with a rifle. Being a storage room, there are boxes everywhere, and they are covered in blood. It's a pretty easy job. We empty the contents of the boxes, place them in new boxes, and throw out the old ones. There is, of course, some blood on parts of walls, on the ceiling, and on a standup mirror that is being stored in there. But all in all it is not too bad.

Shawn moves the mirror to one side to see how much mess there is behind it.

With a lot of private jobs where Crime Scene Cleaners have been called by a victim's family, as opposed to a motel manager, there is a family member present, or at least hovering around to keep an eye on the cleaners. At this job we have a tall Italian-looking guy in jeans and a leather jacket. He doesn't say much. He just hovers around, smoking cigarettes.

"You might not want to see this," says Shawn as he stands up from behind the mirror and turns toward the disposal bag. In his hand, quite unmistakably, is half a brain. It's bloody and messy, but still clearly visible for what it is— *half a brain*!

The family member and I jar against each other in the doorway. Pretty quickly we find ourselves doubled over with about ten yards between us as we throw up in the gutter. His problem is my old problem. He has nothing to throw up. My cheeseburger and fries come up at pretty much the same speed it probably took to make them. Of course, there is some dry retching after this, but the initial, more powerful retches were reduced by stomach content.

The McDonald's, I feel, was a very smooth move.

"Sorry!" Shawn calls out from the doorway.

It's a few minutes before I can go back in and help Shawn with the rest of the job.

"Are you okay?" he asks.

"Yeah, let's just get the fuck out of here," I say, picking up a brush and going to work on the wall. I work hard and fast. My new attitude toward the blood, toward this suicide, is that I want to be somewhere else, and the blood is in my way. The quicker I clean it, the quicker I can be somewhere else. It's that simple. There is no more vomiting, not even a retch. I feel annoyed now, annoyed at the blood, and I don't want one drop of it to survive.

The job is done in little over an hour. On the way out, Shawn and I stop at McDonald's, and I eat my second cheeseburger meal of the day. But something has changed in me. I have crossed a boundary. No matter what the rest of the day has in store for me, I know this cheeseburger will not see the light of day ever again.

MAN IN THE BATH PART IV

The court transcript I have been reading is formatted very much like a film script. It is missing certain elements, like direction: "Lawyer enters from left—looks longingly at judge." But the dialogue is set out with the speaker's name in bold font. It seems a little risky to me, the similarity in the two formats. It's another blurred line between reality and entertainment. As I read I sometimes forget that these are real people discussing a real event. They end up as characters on a page and little more. But something sits uncomfortably in my mind as I read. Because there is no movement and gesture in the court transcript, the characters have no life; they're hard to get off the page.

Shortly after Jim McKinnon was arrested, journalist Ed Walsh visited him in jail and interviewed him. He is called as a witness for the prosecution. This is where, this time sitting in a café in a nice comfy chair with a pile of pancakes,

I pick up on my reading of the court transcript. It reads as follows.

THE CLERK: Please be seated. Please state your name and spell your name for the record, please."

THE WITNESS: Ed Walsh, W-A-L-S-H.

THE JUDGE: Thank you, Mr. Walsh. I'll ask you to please make sure you let the lawyers finish their questions before you answer so only one person is talking at one time.

Please make sure that you answer with words because the court reporter can't take down gestures or "mm-hmms," and please make sure you speak loudly enough so everyone can hear.

All right? Thank you. Mr. Beckelman . . .

MR. BECKELMAN: Your Honor, I'm conscious of what's known as the Press Shield under Evidence Code 1070, and my intent in asking questions will be limited to the four corners of a newspaper article which has been marked as People's Exhibit 19.

I am aware of the case law which does not allow me to ask about any unnamed sources or any unnamed material or unpublished material that this reporter might have collected, and I'm referring specifically to a case called *Hammarley,* H-A-M-M-A-R-L-E-Y, *versus Superior Court,* at 89 CAL.App.3d, 388–397, and "unpublished information" includes notes and summaries of interviews with murder eyewitnesses, and that's within the scope.

So I am limited to just the four corners of the newspaper article, and that is how I would intend to conduct my direct examination of this witness.

MR. OLSON: Your Honor, if I may, Carl Olson, representing the witness.

I appreciate Mr. Beckelman's statement that he will not attempt to go beyond the four corners of the article, and we will object to anything that does go beyond the four corners of the article.

DEPUTY PUBLIC DEFENDER FELDMAN: Judge, I have two concerns: The first one is a discovery problem.

By way of offer of proof, the court is essentially going to be presented with a confession coming through Mr. Walsh's voice. This is my reading of Evidence Code Section 1054.1 a violation of Subsection (b), which requires the prosecution to hand over to me all statements of the defendant's.

It also requires the prosecution to turn over relevant written or recorded statements or reports of witnesses upon whom the prosecutor intends to call to trial.

So the first problem we've got is we've got a discovery problem. I have not been given any notes, I have not been given any background material on what this gentleman is going to testify to.

THE JUDGE: Mr. Beckelman, do the People have any such material?

MR. BECKELMAN: No, we don't, Your Honor.

MR. FELDMAN: Judge, the court has got the Haight and Cotchett book in front of you. I would cite you on the matter, 18—Section 18, Page 149, that says:

"The Shield law does not provide a sweeping privilege against disclosure, but merely an immunity from contempt for failure to disclose. Therefore, the argument that Section 1070 prohibits a discovery order requiring disclosure of reporter's notes is without merit."

THE JUDGE: The basis there is that Section 1054 and the other criminal discovery statutes go to the material in the State's possession; not material that the State does not control.

To the extent that you're seeking material that third parties have, you're required to proceed by way of subpoena, as opposed to the criminal discovery statutes. And that, of course, would provide a forum in which to litigate any problems with respect to that. So the discovery argument is overruled.

MR. FELDMAN: Judge, I'm going to raise a further concern then, if I can have a moment please.

[Pause in the proceedings.]

MR. FELDMAN: I'm going to raise a further concern, Judge, which is that there may be government action involved in the interview of my client by Mr. Walsh. What I am going by are a couple of instances in the newspaper article itself where there has clearly been contact between the investigating officers in this police report and Mr. Walsh. So my concern is that there is government action involved in the taking of this statement.

THE JUDGE: Mr. Beckelman?

MR. BECKELMAN: I have no information of that. I asked Inspector Pera and I will represent to the court that she was not an agent. I asked the same thing of Mr. Walsh just in the hallway, and he laughed.

So if there was any of that, I'm not aware of it.

THE JUDGE: Mr. Beckelman, if you would like to proceed.

MR. BECKELMAN: Thank you.

DIRECT EXAMINATION

MR. BECKELMAN: I would like to hand you what's been marked People's 19 and show it to you and ask whether you recognize it?

THE WITNESS: It's a copy of the Bay Area Reporter from October third, 2002.

MR. BECKELMAN: And did you write an article for that newspaper?

THE WITNESS: Yes.

MR. BECKELMAN: And for that article did you interview a James McKinnon?

THE WITNESS: Yes.

MR. BECKELMAN: And do you see James McKinnon here in the courtroom?

THE WITNESS: Yes. He's wearing an orange sweat suit.

THE JUDGE: The record may reflect the witness has identified the defendant.

MR. BECKELMAN: Did you ask Mr. McKinnon questions about the death of Gary Lee Ober?

THE WITNESS: Yes.

MR. BECKELMAN: Did you ask him whether he was forced to kill Mr. Ober?

MR. FELDMAN: Objection! Leading!

THE JUDGE: Overruled!

THE WITNESS: (No response.)

MR. BECKELMAN: The question began: Did you ask Mr. McKinnon whether he was forced to kill Ober?

THE WITNESS: I don't recall if I used those exact words, if he was forced to kill Mr. Ober, but I did ask him if he killed Mr. Ober.

MR. BECKELMAN: And what did he say?

THE WITNESS: He said he killed him in self-defense.

MR. BECKELMAN: Did he tell you where this homicide or this killing took place?

THE WITNESS: He said it was in the apartment that he was briefly living in—Mr. Ober's apartment. He had been living there when this happened.

MR. BECKELMAN: Did he tell you how he came to be living in Mr. Ober's apartment?

THE WITNESS: He said he was homeless, and that he was friends with Mr. Ober and Mr. Ober agreed to let him stay with him.

MR. BECKELMAN: Did you ask why he had to resort to killing a man 20 years older than him?

THE WITNESS: Yes.

MR. BECKELMAN: And what did he say?

THE WITNESS: He explained that he was very vulnerable at the time, he was very sick, and that Mr. Ober was taking advantage of him at a period of weakness, physical weakness. And so even though Mr. Ober was older, he was the weaker because he was sick.

MR. BECKELMAN: Did you ask him how many days when he

killed him in relation to when he began living with Mr. Ober?

THE WITNESS: He said he had been living with Mr. Ober for three days, you know, before this happened.

MR. BECKELMAN: Did you ask him if he used any weapons in killing Mr. Ober?

THE WITNESS: Yes.

MR. BECKELMAN: Did you ask specifically about a knife?

THE WITNESS: He said he—something to the effect that he didn't know anything about a knife.

MR. BECKELMAN: Do you recall writing or him answering you and you writing, quote: "I don't know why anyone is talking about a knife for I don't know nothing about no knife. I really don't. I did not use any weapons at all. I was sitting on the damn toilet."?

THE WITNESS: Yeah, I was very careful to quote him exactly what he said on my tape.

MR. BECKELMAN: Did you point out to him that Ober's body—that it was reported to you that Ober's body was found sprinkled with baking soda in an attempt to mask the smell?

THE WITNESS: Yes.

MR. BECKELMAN: And what did he say?

THE WITNESS: He said something to the effect that he didn't want to comment on that, I believe.

MR. BECKELMAN: Did you ask him—did you ask him if he went to the police?

THE WITNESS: Yes.

MR. BECKELMAN: And what did he say?

THE WITNESS: "No."

MR. BECKELMAN: Did he tell you why he did not go to the police?

THE WITNESS: He said he was a human being, and he was scared, and he said, "It doesn't matter what happens to me."

MR. BECKELMAN: Did you ask him about a report that you were aware of that he allegedly said to a customer at the Pendulum Bar about him doing a bad thing? Did you ask him about that?

THE WITNESS: Yes.

MR. BECKELMAN: And what did he say?

THE WITNESS: He said he didn't remember if he said that or

not, if he did, it could mean a lot of things. It could mean that he, you know, spilled something or, you know, I think the example he gave is peeing somewhere on something accidentally.

MR. BECKELMAN: That was the analogy he gave?

THE WITNESS: Yeah.

MR. BECKELMAN: Let me ask you this, Mr. Walsh. You were employed as a journalist when you conducted this interview with Mr. McKinnon?

THE WITNESS: Yes.

MR. BECKELMAN: And where did this interview take place?

THE WITNESS: In the San Francisco County Jail.

MR. BECKELMAN: And did you go to the county jail at the direction or the request of the San Francisco Police Department?

THE WITNESS: No.

MR. BECKELMAN: Thank you very much. I have no further questions.

THE JUDGE: Thank you. Mr. Feldman, cross-examination.

MR. FELDMAN: Thank you, Judge.

CROSS-EXAMINATION

MR. FELDMAN: Good afternoon, Mr. Walsh.

THE WITNESS: Hello.

MR. FELDMAN: The interview took place in the county jail on the sixth floor of this building, right?

THE WITNESS: Yes.

MR. FELDMAN: How did you know where Mr. McKinnon was?

THE WITNESS: Well, I knew from reading articles in the press, not mine, but I think it was the <u>Chronicle</u> article mentioned that he was in custody, and so I came to the jail to see if he was here.

MR. FELDMAN: What jail did you go to see if he was here?

THE WITNESS: I went to this one first.

MR. FELDMAN: There are several jails at the Hall of Justice.

THE WITNESS: I believe—you know, I don't really recall. I think I went to—I may have gone to the sixth floor first or I may have gone to the one at 7th Street first, but either way, I was directed to the correct prison he was at.

MR. FELDMAN: You spoke with a deputy somewhere to try and find out where he was in custody, right?

THE WITNESS: You know, I honestly don't recall if I just lucked out and happened to be at the jail he was at, or if I spoke to a deputy first at the wrong jail and they directed me to the right jail. I don't really remember.

MR. FELDMAN: Did you review any kind of jail records?

THE WITNESS: No.

MR. FELDMAN: At some point you did speak to Inspector Pera, right?

THE WITNESS: I spoke with her on the phone, yeah.

MR. FELDMAN: Did you interview any other police officers or did you speak with any other police officers in this case?

THE WITNESS: Yes, I believe that there was another officer that I spoke with . . .

MR. FELDMAN: And who was that?

THE WITNESS: . . . early on. I don't recall.

MR. FELDMAN: How did you reach that officer?

THE WITNESS: By telephone.

MR. FELDMAN: How did you know to call that officer?

THE WITNESS: I was just checking on the story, and I called—

I don't recall which officer that I spoke with, but it was some-body at San Francisco Police Department that gave me some basic information on the case early on.

MR. FELDMAN: And is that before you spoke with Mr. McKinnon?

THE WITNESS: Yes.

MR. FELDMAN: Your interview with Inspector Pera, was that before you spoke with Mr. McKinnon?

THE WITNESS: I believe that was after.

MR. FELDMAN: Your article concludes with a request that anybody having information about this case should call the San Francisco Police Homicide Department; is that right?

THE WITNESS: Yes.

MR. FELDMAN: Why did you put that in your article?

THE WITNESS: It's just something that I discussed with my editor, and I think our thinking was for anybody with in-formation on either side of the case, whether it be pro or con, pro defense or whatever, or pro prosecution, for people to come forward. I think it's in the interest of the commu-nity for people with information on a crime to come for-ward.

MR. FELDMAN: So in other words, a neutral request?

THE WITNESS: Yes.

MR. FELDMAN: Would you say that your article is written in a neutral fashion?

MR. BECKELMAN: Objection.

MR. OLSON: Objection. Irrelevant.

THE JUDGE: Sustained.

MR. FELDMAN: How would we know when you spoke with Inspector Pera? How would we get that piece of information?

MR. BECKELMAN: Objection, relevance.

THE JUDGE: Sustained.

MR. FELDMAN: The other officer that you spoke with, that was before you went to see Mr. McKinnon, right?

THE WITNESS: Yes.

MR. FELDMAN: And did you discuss any specifics of the case with that officer?

THE WITNESS: Just the basic, you know, details, what, where, when. You know, just the basics of the case.

MR. FELDMAN: Was that officer involved in the investigation of the case?

THE WITNESS: I don't recall if that officer was or if he was just somebody in the public affairs department that was giving the information.

MR. FELDMAN: When you went into the jail did the Sheriff's deputies . . . Were they aware that you had a tape deck?

THE WITNESS: I don't know if they were or not.

MR. FELDMAN: You're aware of the rules that say you can't take any kind of thing into the jail?

MR. BECKELMAN: Objection, relevance.

THE JUDGE: Sustained.

MR. FELDMAN: You have some information in this report, for instance, coming from a guy by the name of Franco, a quote about Mr. McKinnon suddenly being flush with money. Did you get that piece of information out of a police report or did that come from an interview with Mr. Franco?

MR. OLSON: OBJECTION, SHIELD LAW.

THE JUDGE: Mr. Feldman?

MR. FELDMAN: Judge, I'm still concerned about government action. I would like to know if this gentleman had a chance to review any police reports prior to going into the jail.

THE JUDGE: Is the suggestion that Mr. Franco is a police officer?

MR. FELDMAN: No, the suggestion is that, by way of offer of proof, it's a direct quote from a police report.

MR. OLSON: My problem with that, Your Honor, is that would fall within the definition of unpublished information under Evidence Code Section 1070, Article 1, Section (2) (b).

THE JUDGE: The objection is sustained.

MR. FELDMAN: Judge, I can't find out about government action if I can't ask this gentleman if he has had the chance to review prior police reports, if anybody gave him that report prior to him speaking with Mr. McKinnon.

THE JUDGE: That would be a different question.

MR. FELDMAN: Did any police officers provide you with any police reports in this case?

THE WITNESS: No.

MR. FELDMAN: Did you review any police reports prior to interviewing Mr. McKinnon?

THE WITNESS: No.

MR. FELDMAN: Mr. McKinnon told you that he was forced to kill Mr. Ober to fend off a sexual assault, right?

THE WITNESS: Yes.

MR. FELDMAN: Mr. McKinnon told you, "It was self-defense, that's all I'm going to say. I was attacked while I was on the toilet," right?

THE WITNESS: That's correct.

MR. FELDMAN: Mr. McKinnon told you at that time he had pneumonia and a temperature of over 102 degrees, right?

THE WITNESS: Yes.

MR. FELDMAN: He told you that when he was assaulted he was on the toilet with his pants down around his ankles, right?

THE WITNESS: Yes.

MR. FELDMAN: He said Mr. Ober let him stay with him because he was homeless, right?

THE WITNESS: Yes.

MR. FELDMAN: And that they were friends and not boyfriends, right?

THE WITNESS: Yes.

MR. FELDMAN: Did Mr. McKinnon say anything to you that struck you as a little bit strange in terms of the way he presented himself to you?

MR. OLSON: Your Honor, I'm going to object to that under Evidence Code Section 1070. I think the witness's mental state, which this is essentially calling for, is also unpublished information.

THE JUDGE: I'll sustain the objection. His mental state, also, I don't think is relevant.

MR. FELDMAN: You asked him why he didn't go to the police, right?

THE WITNESS: Yes.

MR. FELDMAN: And he told you that he was just a human being and that he's scared, right?

THE WITNESS: Yes.

MR. FELDMAN: Did he make any biblical references to you?

THE WITNESS: Yes, I believe he did.

MR. FELDMAN: Something to the extent, "It doesn't matter what happens to me," that, "There's a plague coming," right? Did he express any paranoia towards the government?

THE WITNESS: I don't recall specifically him expressing paranoia, but . . .

MR. FELDMAN: He told you that the government has done

more wrong in five minutes than he has done in his entire life, right?

THE WITNESS: Yeah, but . . .

MR. FELDMAN: Yes or no?

THE WITNESS: Yes.

MR. FELDMAN: And he talked about Saddam Hussein, right?

THE WITNESS: Yes.

MR. FELDMAN: And he talked about Bin Laden, right?

THE WITNESS: Yes.

MR. FELDMAN: I've got nothing further. Thank you, sir.

THE JUDGE: Thank you, Mr. Walsh. You may step down.

[The witness stands down.]

THE JUDGE: Did the defense wish to present any evidence today?

MR. FELDMAN: We're not going to be presenting any evidence, Judge.

THE JUDGE: All right. Mr. Beckelman, did you wish to address the charge?

MR. BECKELMAN: Subject to rebuttal.

THE JUDGE: Mr. Feldman, did you wish to address the charge?

MR. FELDMAN: The court has heard competent evidence that Mr. McKinnon was inside 182 Bemis at a time that there most likely was a corpse inside 182 Bemis. That's 95 percent of what we talked about was.

Then we got this, we got a report from a reporter acting surreptitiously. He's not allowed to take a tape deck in there, and that's a confession, and the entire evidence of a murder is based on what Mr. Walsh told us.

There was no evidence of a murder before . . .

THE JUDGE: That's not true. I mean we have Dr. Stephens telling us that it was a homicide, and that there were knife wounds, and that his opinion is that that's what the cause of death was.

MR. FELDMAN: Let me change that. The only evidence that Mr. McKinnon murdered Mr. Ober came out of this man's mouth based on an interview where Mr. McKinnon sounds paranoid, sounds scared, he's talking about the Bible, he's talking about the government. That shouldn't be enough to hold him to answer.

I will submit it.

THE JUDGE: All right. Mr. McKinnon, would you please rise, sir?

[The defendant stands.]

THE JUDGE: Mr. McKinnon, the court has heard the evidence presented today and I've considered the argument of counsel.

Let me say first of all, I'm sympathetic to counsel's frustration in being presented with the task of having to cross-examine with respect to what he's characterized as a confession without additional information.

I know that's an issue that will be litigated further. I don't know ultimately whether that confession will survive for trial. That's an issue that will be tested down the road. But there is evidence before me today that Mr. Ober was murdered, that you were the one there, both at the relevant times, that you continued to be there for at least a few weeks, if not longer, after the murder occurred with the body in the tub and, of course, I also have evidence in front of me that you admitted killing Mr. Ober.

So for all those reasons, it appears to the court that from the production of satisfactory evidence that a crime of felony has been committed; specifically, a violation of Penal Code Section 187, and there is reasonable and probable cause to believe that you are guilty of that offense, it is now the order of this court that you be held for trial before the Superior Court of the State of California in and for the City and County of San Francisco.

I have mixed feelings as I read the judge's summary. Not about McKinnon coming to trial; as the judge said, there is probable cause to believe that McKinnon is guilty of the crime. I feel mixed because I am glad that McKinnon is being brought to trial, but disappointed that the transcript has come to an end and that I have no definite conclusion to the story.

As I close the transcript I find myself instantly digging my cell phone out of my pocket. I am all of a sudden overwhelmed by the idea of attending the trial. There's a part of me, having worked my way through this story via Shawn of Crime Scene Cleaners, Inspectors Toomey and Pera, and now the preliminary transcript, that finds myself wanting to see McKinnon in the flesh. To watch him answer for the crime.

MISS MISERY

On average, 2.5 million people die every year in America. Just fewer than 20,000 of those will be murdered, whereas some 32,500 people will commit suicide. That's one person every seventeen minutes. For every successful suicide there are eight other attempts. Women attempt suicide more than men, but five times the number of men succeed in taking their own lives. The main determinants of suicide are depression, alcohol abuse, narcotics use, and separation or divorce. The most popular way to commit suicide is with a firearm. There are roughly 17,000 firearm suicides every year, which account for 52 percent of the suicide rate. The most up-to-date stats show that for the year recorded, 5,744 people poisoned themselves with drugs and other substances in a bid to end their lives, and 7,248 people chose suffocation or hanging. Second from last comes cutting or piercing, with 590 suicides. Finally, drowning accounted for 375 people in the recorded year.

Since hanging around with the Crime Scene Cleaners, I have been giving serious thought to the choice of method by which people put an end to their own lives, and what these methods say about them.

With a firearm you know you are going to leave an awful mess for somebody to find. Of course, you can choose to carry out this act at home, at work, or at a lover's, but you could just as well drive into the woods, where you will likely be found by strangers walking their dogs. But, on the whole, suicides by gun seem not to have any consideration for what will be left behind or who will find that mess. It seems that the finality of a gun to the head outweighs all other concerns. When I say finality, of course, now and again people do miss. In general, however, by placing a gun against your head, or against the roof of your mouth, and pulling the trigger, you can be pretty sure of your success. So it could be argued that suicide by gun is first and foremost all about securing your outcome. There is a visual aspect, but I don't think that is the overriding factor in the decision. Such decisions are born out of pain and the overwhelming desire to put a stop to it immediately. But the reality isn't always so.

In fact, people often survive suicide when trying to shoot themselves in the temple or through the mouth. The recoil of the gun is rarely considered, especially by those unused to handling firearms. The recoil often redirects the aim, so people end up removing portions of their frontal lobe and still live, some to tell the tale, others to sit vegetating as a symbol of the act.

Hanging is a different kettle of fish. I can't help but see hanging as theater. Sure, death rules the day, but by choosing hanging you have considered the visual aspect of your statement. You are not leaving just the mark of death but a complete and well-composed scene. Because hanging is as much about the preparation and presentation as it is the final result of death. You form an idea of how it should look before you even begin on practicalities. That image is likely to be of an entire room, not just noose, neck, and tongue. Only once you have that wide-angle image, might you start to look around for a suitable beam. What will you use for a rope? It should be strong, of course; you wouldn't want it to break. (Or would you? It is theater, after all.) You'll place a chair in the middle of the room and check the height against your noose. You might at that point step down and smoke a cigarette, drink a whiskey, maybe not, but you will give thought to the reaction of the person who will find you: that's the whole reason for your chosen method. You are playing to an audience of one and generally try to time it so that nobody but the chosen will find you.

Even though as a method it is relatively clean, hanging is not about the avoidance of mess, it is about visual drama. It's a photograph that will never fade. Once you have the stage set just so, you will step up to the noose, tighten it around your neck, and kick away the chair. There's an element of vanity in hanging: you are a showman and you are not so much having the last word as posing the final question.

In fact, that is what a hanged body often looks like, with its snapped neck and slightly bent legs: a dead question mark.

Hanging seems terribly unfair. You pose the final question while at the same time telling the viewer that he or she is too late. The person may have the answer but the buzzer has gone. Live with it.

Hanging is also popular as a cry for help. People set the stage and then wait by the window for their audience to arrive. A friend once relayed a personal story regarding a family member who admitted to planning it this way. It made me think of surprise birthday parties. I couldn't get beyond the, "She's here/he's here/it's now" moment.

Surpriiiise!

Poison by carbon monoxide, on the other hand, is completely without pomp. It's quiet, mundane even, but, most important, it is incredibly adult and mature. I can't get away from the fact that poison, especially in a car, is the only true form of suicide. It is just about you, you and death, and in that decision all is calm. It's calm because of all the methods, carbon-monoxide poisoning comes with a get-out clause that lasts into the process.

With shooting, you do not start the actual process of killing yourself until you pull the trigger, and then it's over (recoil permitting) in a flash. With hanging, the process of death begins not with the preparation but when you kick the stool away; it may not be over in a flash, but there is little you can do once the creaking starts. With suffocation by car fumes, the process of killing yourself starts when you close the car door and start the engine. Even with an old carbon-monoxide-producing heap of a car, you will be conscious for a couple of minutes. The process is in motion, but you can open the door and jump out at any time. Sure, you will need medical attention—carbon-monoxide poisoning is very serious—but there is still some time allotted to act on any doubt.

Carbon-monoxide poisoning is not, like is often believed, clean. It may not even be painless. When carbon monoxide is inhaled, it takes the place of oxygen in the hemoglobin, the red blood pigment that normally carries oxygen to all parts of the body. Carbon monoxide binds to hemoglobin up to several hundred times more strongly than oxygen, and its effects are cumulative and long-lasting, causing oxygen starvation throughout the body. At 6,400 parts per million (0.64 percent), headaches and dizziness come in one to two minutes. Death in less than twenty minutes. But at what point do you pass out? This is hard to record and an unethical experiment. But the effects on the body due to this poisoning are severe and have been reported to include swollen tongues, ruptured capillaries, and burst eyeballs.

Cutting, wrist cutting in particular, strikes me as being closely linked to hanging. It is a visual communication, but one slightly more aggressive than hanging. Neal described it as ". . . the final 'fuck you' to everyone around you."

I think he is right. But it is a prolonged "fuck you." Death is not instant: if you choose to cut your wrists as a means to death, you are in no great rush. You are not looking for instant death: on the contrary, you want to feel life ebbing out of you.

Wrist cutting is also artistic.

There is no denying that it is visually striking. Unless you are going to get up really close, what you are going to see is a body relaxing in a bath of red water, maybe with the arms hanging outside and some blood on the floor. As a piece of art it conjures up something sacrificial. The point being made is not one-upmanship; it's not about right or wrong, it's about being superior. "I am better than this, I am better than you, and so I have moved on. Stay put, schmuck!"

The statement is aesthetic. It is final, undiluted, and as

an image it remains cemented in the mind of whoever finds you.

Building jumpers are looking for something else. They are going out with a rush, riddled with sensation. Then it's over. Simple as that. One minute you're flying, then you're not. It's a bit like flicking a switch.

Train jumpers I do not get. What are they thinking? How is jumping in front of a train a serious option for people wanting to die? It's not guaranteed and certainly not painless. I have interviewed police officers and firemen in New York City who told stories of train jumpers who actually ended up under the trains, mangled, but alive. It's common that these people get twisted and bound up and are held together by the pressure of the train pinning them in place. Only once the train is moved do they spill out and die. One officer even told me of a case when they didn't move the train until a loved one had arrived to say good-bye.

I can't see any statement with such suicides, unless it is despair. Maybe in a flash you are overcome with rage (dare I say against the machine?) and take a running jump at the nearest symbol of a frustrated life.

Maybe it is connected to strength, or a lack of it. Maybe you want to die but can't go all the way. You can manage only 70 percent of the job and need somebody else to see it through. Maybe you are putting the responsibility in somebody else's hands, making him or her complicit in your demise.

I remember reading about a woman in Devon, England, who had sat waiting at a bus stop. As the bus went into gear and began to pull away she dashed over, knelt down, and stuck her head in front of the back wheel. She had wanted to die, for sure, but had not the means to carry it out. The most she could do was put herself in death's path.

The most expensive suicide I read about in my research was that of Air Force Captain Craig Button, who (according to the official report released by the air force) killed himself by flying his A-10 fighter plane into the thirteen-thousand-foot Gold Dust Peak in Colorado.

The A-10 Thunderbolt costs $9.8 million.

If I ever decided that the game was up, an A-10 would suit me just dandy. But if I didn't have access to an A-10 Thunderbolt, I am certain I would want the least painful and the least messy option available.

Neal, of course, would not want to hear these words. If I were to start promoting my clean method of suicide he would be bankrupt in no time at all. (On reflection, this isn't true. He would definitely outmarket me and outwork me.) If Neal were to have a suicide-advice line, it would be on the best way to do it—*for him*. He would certainly recommend the shotgun as the de rigueur option, double barreled, preferably with you in the center of the room.

"Okay, so now you've got your shotgun loaded. Take a seat in your armchair . . ."

A good friend of mine used to work in a large bookshop in Piccadilly, London. When I say big, I mean six floors and half a million books. The exterior and interior of this bookshop are beautiful and a reason to visit in themselves. Inside, there's a big set of stairs that wind their way around an atrium. It's the atrium that sticks in my mind, because I remember clearly the day when Sean called me and said, "You won't believe what's just happened here: a customer just climbed to the top floor and took a dive down the stairwell."

Apparently, after colliding with an art nouveau chandelier, the man proceeded to bounce and crash all the way down to the marble floor in the basement. He died on site.

No connection was ever made between the man and Waterstone's Books, and the retailer was in no way accountable. The stairwell had a high railing; the man had dragged over a chair and had stood on it in order to clear the banister.

I remember thinking that it was a strange place to kill yourself. I mean, what is it he was trying to say? Why a bookshop? Why this bookshop? Who was the audience? I wanted to know this stuff. I didn't want to accept that the location was meaningless.

It had to mean something. Tell me it was a protest against a complacent middle class, in particular. Tell me it was a protest against deforestation, or against one particular book.

I remember talking to Sean a couple of weeks later and asking, "Did you ever hear why that man committed suicide in your shop?"

"No; it seems there was no connection to Waterstone's or the location itself. It's bizarre," he told me. "But amongst the staff here we have settled on the suicide as being the ultimate form of criticism."

So this strange event passed without there really being any knowledge as to why this man chose to commit suicide, or why he chose such a location and method. The easy assumption is that he was depressed, that is the word that most often gets thrown around with suicide. But what about the idea of completion? Suicide is the only way you can complete your story on your terms. If what you are after is total control, then suicide is a must.

There's also shame. Death in itself is the ultimate form of escapism. You could get caught in your local village copulating with a farm animal, the shame of which would probably lead you to escape to another town, far, far away from past furry romances. But what happens when the shame is on a much grander scale? Take former Enron executive J. Clifford Baxter, for example, who shot himself through the right side of the head while sitting in his Mercedes. Baxter was reportedly unhappy with Enron practices and ultimately resigned as vice chairman (though he stayed on as a consultant). He had made over twenty million dollars from Enron stocks in the years leading up to the scandal and bankruptcy. He was named in a shareholder lawsuit, was subpoenaed by the congressional committee investigating the Enron affair, and was expected to give evidence.

In his suicide note he wrote to his wife, Carol, ". . . where there was once great pride now it's gone."

When it came to escapism, Baxter didn't just head to the next town over; he escaped to the farthest possible destination.

Freud wrote that as humans we are driven by two conflicting fundamental desires: the life drive, which concerns itself with survival (reproduction, hunger, thirst, and sex) and the death drive. The death drive represents an intrinsic urge in all of us to return to a state of calm: to an inorganic or dead state. The death drive moves us toward extreme pleasure, which in Freud's opinion is a state of nothingness; it's the result of a complete reduction in stimuli, the state a body enters after having been exposed to extremity. Pushed by chaos and noise, sought out by our own desires, any one of us could make the leap to calmer waters. Any one of us is capable of suicide and actually has a built-in desire for the peace it would bring.

In *The Myth of Sisyphus,* Albert Camus introduces his philosophy of the absurd: man's futile search for meaning and clarity in the face of an unintelligible world. He poses what he considers to be the only real philosophical question that matters: does the realization of the meaninglessness and absurdity of life require suicide?

He concludes by comparing the absurdity of modern man's life with that of Sisyphus, a figure in Greek mythology who was condemned to a lifetime of repeatedly pushing a rock up a mountain, only to see it roll down again. Camus concludes, "The struggle itself . . . is enough to fill a man's heart. One must imagine Sisyphus happy."

The conclusion is that the realization of the absurd does not require suicide; quite the opposite, by accepting the absurd we are spared and are rewarded with happiness.

It's those who question the meaninglessness of life generally, of their own lives specifically, who are edging nearer to suicide, nearer to Neal Smither and his band of merry men.

Neal has mastered the absurdity of life. He is Sisyphus. He wakes up each day, kisses his wife and child good-bye, and goes to work, washing away the blood and brains of the previous day's departures. He comes home, eats dinner, goes to sleep, and wakes up in the morning with the prospect of washing away the blood and brains of the previous day's departures. I am convinced that Neal will live happily until natural death takes him gently away.

MISCREANTS ON THE LOOSE

It's eleven A.M. when my phone rings, and I already have a pen in my hand when I answer.

"Alan—Neal. What's up, buddy?"

"I'm good."

"You up?"

"Sure am."

"You have fun yesterday?"

"Yeah, I did. I mean, to be honest with you, I was just relieved that something happened. I was starting to worry that I wouldn't get enough for my book. But that's terrible and I—"

"*Dude,* never worry. It always comes. You just gotta keep praying for death. And you were praying like a motherfucker, weren't you?"

"Yeah, I was. But, Neal . . . shit. That's just *awful*. I mean, I really was, but I feel a bit messed up right now. . . ."

"Oh, Alan, *fuck it*. This shit happens without you. They

didn't die because you wanted your story. They just fucking *died*. Don't get yourself all wet over it. Anyway, listen, I got a nice one for you. You still want it?"

Once again I am with Shawn, standing in the middle of the most awful mess. But this is nothing like the continuous dripping of a slit wrist, or the splatter from a shotgun.

"Apparently," Shawn tells me, "it was drink. I suppose he just drank until his liver burst."

The house is a typical, big, middle-class multiroomed thing in the middle of a street lined with big, middle-class houses. The room in which the bulk of the problem exists was clearly not a pretty sight before it was coated in blood. You can smell the alcohol everywhere, although most of that is coming from the blood. Every surface, the corners of the room, and the adjoining bathroom are filled with beer bottles, wine bottles, and liquor bottles.

There is little information available for this job. We do know that the victim was twenty-four years old. We know that the parents were on vacation—*are still on vacation*. There is no mention as to whether the boy had a long history of drinking, but looking at all these bottles lined up like trophies, or like notches in a countdown, he clearly must have done. Even a half-wit would know that drinking in such large quantities is going to lead to death in the short run. If this was his thinking, I mean if he consciously decided to keep drinking until he died, what an awful state of mind he must have been in.

I stand here hoping he didn't know; hoping he was just on some kind of twenty-four-hour party-crazed drink binge. At least that way he didn't know. At least that way he wasn't in the most terrible mental pain. People should not be left to get into a state where they drink themselves to death, no matter what the history. Even though that is what it looks and smells like, with all these bottles and all this blood, like he did intentionally drink himself to death, I hope it wasn't so.

I didn't think anything could make more of a mess than a shotgun, but deaths like this one are not instant. You can see by the fact that the blood leads all the way through the house and down to the basement, to the wine cellar, that this person was alive for a while after the liver burst.

When the cleaners are out in their trucks, or taking lunch with their Crime Scene Cleaners T-shirts on, people stop them in admiration. "Wow, you see a lot of blood! How many jobs do you do? How can you clean . . . ?" But with jobs like this there really isn't that much actual cleaning. The bedroom and everything in it is a mess. The neighbor, who is phoning back and forth with the parents, who are a twenty-four-hour flight away, has agreed that everything should be thrown out. Everything is, after all, caked in blood. So the bed sheets, the quilt, the carpet, the drawers, the clothes, anything that is removable is indeed removed and stuffed into a bin bag or wrapped in plastic. We will be stripping carpet and furniture from his room, the sister's room, the parents' room, the laundry room, and all the carpet from the spiral staircase.

"At the end of the day, we're just glorified janitors," Shawn says. "People are just in awe because of the blood."

After a short spell of silence, I hear Shawn walk into the bedroom and turn the television on. I am trying to remember

the television. I have an image of the television and find myself wondering if the image I have in my mind's eye is accu-
rate. I walk back into the bedroom and take a look.

Yep. I had it pretty much spot on.

"Shawn?" I call out. "The television screen is covered in
blood."

Of course he knows this, but I feel a need to reiterate it.

"Dude, I'm not going to watch it. I just thought we'd listen to the news while we worked."

My natural reflex reaction is to think, *Shawn, that's
fucked up!* But as I look around the room, I remember that
there is great need for Shawn. I can see why and how you
have to separate yourself. A part of me feels relief that
Shawn is here; that Neal exists and had the foresight to start
this company. I don't care how they deal with it mentally,
just as long as they are here to deal with it. As long as this
heartrending scene is cleaned up before the parents arrive,
who cares how desensitized they are?

"Do you think you'll ever go back to art, Shawn?" I call
out from my enzyme duties in the bathroom.

"Oh, *absolutely*; I don't see why not. You know I still, and
this is morbid, but you know, there's times when we'll go and
pull a chunk of carpet out and there'll be a guy's perfect
imprint—like a body, a perfect print, and all I wanna do is just
cut it out and frame it. You know, I mean almost like Warhol-
ish. I wouldn't even put a brushstroke to it . . . it's just gorgeous. A gorgeous, morbid soul. But at the same time, I can't,
right now at least, see myself doing anything other than what
I do now. I mean, I love my job."

"What is it you love about the job?"

"Well, I get to meet a huge cross-section of life; death

doesn't discriminate. I meet the white trash and the million-aires. And also, yeah, I believe people need us, and that we take away the gore of death. We remove the visual element, which means they don't have to physically touch their grief on top of trying to deal with it mentally. We help them grieve. Like this job. Should the parents come home and find their son like this? This mess? This smell? They're coming back right now, but isn't the loss of their son enough? What we do in a lot of situations saves a lot of pain, a lot of heartbreak. Then sometimes it doesn't, but, you know, people don't want to face this stuff and mom and dad don't wanna face this stuff and I do, I guess, so it's good for everyone in the end."

I understand that the work of Crime Scene Cleaners spares loved ones hurt and pain, but it also spares some of them guilt. If you felt you had played a part in a loved one's demise, that you had not been there for him or her in life when you should have been, you could be expected to feel guilt. Imagine how that guilt could spiral if you then had to clean them up?

Neal was right: while you can't schedule it on a daily basis, death doesn't really fall behind on the overall numbers. It's ten P.M. and I am racing over the Bay Bridge. As soon as Neal told me about the job, my heart began racing. I haven't even put my shoes on yet or stopped for coffee.

For the first time in my life, I find myself speeding toward a fresh murder scene and once again living a contradiction. I am excited. I know I shouldn't be. If a friend were here I would try to hide my enthusiasm. In fact, were anybody here whom I respect, I would try to hide myself.

Can it really be death that has me all pumped up? Maybe, though I don't think so. I think it is more closely connected with this being so far away from my normal life. It is connected to a fantasy. Not necessarily one of my own creating. It's one put there by Hollywood, and I am not blaming Hollywood for that. That would be too cheap. Nobody made me watch the film *Seven,* and still to this day I think it is one of the best thrillers I have ever seen. If it were on at the cinema now I'd go and see it again. I love good thrillers. The fact that I am right now in my rental car racing to a homicide means that I am a step closer to the fantasy and excitement of a good thriller. I still feel coarse and crass. I know that it is not really okay. This after all is not fantasy. It is not a thriller. What I write may be entertainment, but it is not Hollywood. It isn't even fiction. It's reality; it's somebody else's sad story, and I seem to be gate-crashing.

All writing is voyeuristic, but it's not all *this* voyeuristic. I am only one sad move away from being an ambulance chaser. I am far worse than Neal. Who was I ever to judge him? Neal isn't a bad guy at all. He is certainly more honest than I. With Neal you get what you get and you get it face-on. Neal, it is plain to see, has a purpose here. A need. Hell, he's even been invited.

I invited myself.

Yet, I am pulled on. Nothing is going to make me turn this car around. Even knowing that the results, my own sad part in this story, the process and drive that makes me of questionable character, are going to be bound in a book for people to read doesn't stop me.

Maybe that's the only way I'll face it. If it remains inside me I don't ever really have to acknowledge it. I can just put my foot down and race from one story to another, hoping that what I will soon stand before is fucked up and interesting enough for other people to want to read about it. The magazine editors I usually work for are hoping so, too. Just today I had an e-mail from an editor asking why I have not offered them any stories in the last few weeks.

"Have you forgotten us?" the e-mail asked.

But by committing this story to paper, by putting it out there in the public domain, I will have to go through a process of self-reflection. People will see. My friends and family will know. I will know they know.

I see I have arrived at the right meeting place when I spot Neal's truck parked under the glare of the gas station forecourt. I park my car and jump into his truck, which instantly lets out a roar and pins me back in the seat as we screech onto the road and speed off through a red light.

When we arrive at the scene, we find that it has already been processed. The public has dispersed and all that's left is one police car. The officer jumps out of his car when we pull up. He shows us what we need to clean. It's a small puddle of blood, about an inch deep and a foot long, in the gutter of the road.

"You need to be quick here, buddy," the officer says to Neal. "We've got a lot a problems tonight."

"Yes, sir," Neal says, on the move. "I'm on it. We'll be outta here in no time."

This area is called the "Iron Triangle" after the railway

tracks that hem it in on three sides. It's about one and a half square miles of project housing—of poverty, gangs, and drugs.

"This is a fucked-up neighborhood," Neal says as he gathers what he needs from the truck. "I'm out here a lot, and I'm telling you, guns are going off all the fucking time here. You just hear them in the distance."

Neal is suited up and soaking the blood with tissue. He has been on his hands and knees for about two minutes when we freeze at the sound of gunshots—two gunshots that stiffen the spine and dry the mouth. It's one thing to be told that guns are going off all the time here, it's quite another to actually hear them for yourself. The gunshots are not on top of us, but the fact that they are within hearing distance is enough. Neal is working fast, fast even for Neal. The police officer continues to stand guard. He won't leave us out here alone; the area is too volatile. That and the fact that the gunman, or gunmen, responsible for the puddle Neal is mopping up is still out there.

Neal goes almost kamikaze with the enzyme canister. Then we jump back into the truck and wheel-spin away after just ten minutes on the job.

"Did you hear the gunshots?" Neal asks with much animation. "That's why they call this place the Iron Triangle. *Motherfucker,* my heart was pounding when I heard those gunshots. I was like, 'Whoa, clean faster, clean faster!' Damn! That was fun, though, wasn't it? We'll probably get the other one, too."

"What other one?" I ask, almost drowning in an adrenaline wave.

"From those other gunshots."

"You think that was another murder?"

"What the fuck do you think? I'd say the odds are in our favor. We get a lot of jobs in Richmond. Guns are going off all the fucking time in this neighborhood! You do *not* wanna live in Richmond."

It's one A.M. and I *am* back in Richmond and we *are* working the other murder. Or maybe just another murder? Who's to know?

What I do know is that chicken, in itself, is not classified as a deadly weapon. That is why I would like to recommend that if you have people coming after you with guns, you arm yourself with something more substantial than a deep-fried drumstick. Certainly, do not pull your car over to the side of the road and start devouring a ten-piece bucket while parked in your own neighborhood. Your focus needs to be not on the greasy bird in the box, but on the gun-wielding maniacs who have designs on putting *you* in a box.

It may sound like one stereotype colliding with another stereotype: two black guys going at a bucket of fried chicken as they are murdered in a gangland shooting, but that *is* the scene. It seems that while these two guys were in midmouthful, somebody walked up to the car and opened fire on them.

The bucket of chicken is now splattered with blood.

Crime Scene Cleaners are not to touch the car. This is a crime scene still being processed. Why are we here, then, if these guys were shot in the car? It's not like we are going to clean the car, after all (not until it goes for auction, that is).

We're here because the passenger had managed to get out of the car. He tried to run for cover.

He didn't make it.

His blood is on the street. Both under the car and leading away from it.

Most of the blood, though, is under the car, and so we have to wait for the processing to finish and for the car to be removed. Shawn goes to talk to the tow-truck driver to see if he knows when he is towing the car.

"Did you hear what the tow-truck driver said to me?" asks Shawn, returning. "He says, like, 'Do you carry a gun?' and I'm like, 'No!' He's like, 'Well, you might wanna start thinking about it,' and I say, 'Nah, that's cool'; and he lifts up his fucking jacket and he's got a gun right there. A total concealed weapon; against the law! I'm here a lot, and when I am I just wanna get in and *out*. Did I tell you about the job I did a few weeks back where the little girl got shot in the head—through the door?"

"No. I think I would remember that."

"They'd been having problems; apparently she was part of some Asian gang, or I think her brothers were. And around midnight some guys came and rang the doorbell or knocked on the door and just, like, kind of ran back to a safe distance, and as soon as the door opened they just opened fire. Two guys. This homicide was announced on the radio station as I was driving to it, like, 'This just in . . .' and when I got there, there was media everywhere. TV cameras from NBC Eleven, KPIX, Channel Five, and some FOX affiliate. And there were lots of other people there like journalists or radio. There was a big glow from them. Big bright lights everywhere, because they're always packed together in the same area. It's always just a mass of lights. But they all have to stay behind the tape. Then I walk up and I lift the tape and step in, ask who's in charge, and, you know, do my thing."

"But how do you know all this about the murder?" I ask. "The story, I mean. From reading the papers the following day?"

"Well, they were pulling bullets from the wall while I was starting the cleanup. We were just chatting, you know. It was actually quite a trip. I mean I was as close to this guy who was digging bullets outta the wall as I am to you now. And then later I saw it on the news and they were like, 'We need to carry this door outta here.' And I was there with them when they were pulling the door off to take it for evidence, right there, just inside, *cleaning*. And then when I saw it on the news it showed them carrying the door off and leaving with it. It was kind of like this weird bubble. It was like, 'This is what the public sees,' and I'm looking at it like, 'There they go,' and on TV it's like, 'Here they come.' And I knew loads of stuff before the press did, 'cause I knew it was two different shooters because I heard them when they found two different bullets. 'Here's a .357 and here's a 9 mm, oh well if it's a 9 mm then we're gonna find shell casings, but if it's a .357 we're not.' You know, they were using all this police jargon. 'But maybe we'll find a 9-mm casing and we'll get a fingerprint, oh look, here's a 9-mm shell.' And they were right there digging into the wall."

We are told that it will be another ten to fifteen minutes before the car at the current murder scene can be moved. There are lots of officers, as well as lots of what appear to be prostitutes, checking out the scene. There are people so screwed up on drugs that it is starting to represent a clip from *Night of the Living Dead*. It really is odd to see these people openly mixing with the police. Of course, they are aware that, for a short time only, they are of little interest to the men with badges and guns. They are on a reprieve and so they get daring.

The prostitutes and junkies, trying to sneak a peek, edge nearer to the car. Closer and closer they go until one of the officers tells them, "Fuck off!" Then they scamper back like cockroaches, wait a couple of minutes, and then slowly, slowly crabwalk in again. Thinking that by shuffling sideways they will go undetected.

And so the scene repeats itself.

" 'Do I ever consider getting myself a gun?' " continues Shawn. "Can you believe that? When your number's up, your number's up. It's like Neal says: 'If you've got a gun you're either gonna use it or it's gonna get used on you.' You know, in the United States, *supposedly,* most gun victims are shot with their own guns. Just look at all the homicides we do, and all the suicides that are done with guns. I mean, do I want a gun? Guess what!"

It's hard to know how many gun owners are killed with their own guns; there are no statistics on this, aside from that the idea stinks of urban myth. But of the twenty thousand-odd murders committed in a year, the statistics available state that roughly 68 percent of them will be committed with firearms, 56 percent of the overall total with handguns. Around eight hundred people die every year from gun-related accidents.

Finally, we are working on cleaning the blood from two of this year's firearm murders. The crowd is smaller now that the victim's car has been towed away, but there are a few people who continue to mill around, and there are still two or three officers on the scene.

"Look at them. They're like fucking hyenas," says Shawn, looking up from his hands and knees at the members of the public who just won't go away. "It's a fucking weird job, dude, I swear to God. 'Cause it's not natural. You know, animals—unless you're a hyena or a vulture or one of those scavengers—mammals and animals as a whole shy away from death. It's a natural instinct to get the hell outta the situation. And we go traipsing in there every fucking day. 'Oh, somebody died in here? Let's go check it out.'"

The next evening I bump into my friend Rachel. Even though I am still living in her house, our paths have not crossed for a couple of days.

"Hey, where've you been?" she asks. "Did you get your dead people?"

"Sure did. Actually, it has been mad; suicides, murders, it's just . . ."

"Oh, cool. I'm so pleased for you," she says sarcastically.

I walk off laughing with her, but the reality is that, well, as I sit down on the futon in the bedroom, my reality comes crashing down. I am unsure of who I have become in this last month, or, in fact, who I was in the first place. I thought I knew. I thought I had a sense of decency. I simply don't know anymore. I have a stabbing suspicion that there is little integrity about me.

When I wake up the next morning I am still in that frame of mind, wondering where this sense of decency went? How can I lose it so quickly after just one month away from my home, from my friends and family? Why am I walking around victorious at my achievement of worming my way into the sadness and loss of other people? To have made so much fun of it?

If I can't understand my own thoughts then how am I to understand the thought process of the woman who checked into a hotel, slipped on a nice dress, did her hair and makeup, and then wrapped her head in a towel and shot herself in the cranium?

This is just terrible.

Yet, here I am, playing my own part in another tragic end. I'm still trying to understand things I have no right to, things I am not even capable of.

Neal says she wrapped the towel around her head so as to create less mess. To soak up the blood.

I can go with that as an explanation. But I will never understand it.

"When she checked in," the motel receptionist tells me as if it is a little tidbit of gossip, "she took her key and said, 'Now I am going to go and kill myself.'"

Enough is enough. I have to get out of here. I have to get away from death. Away from people who make their living from death. I want to go home and write. Write *my* book, which will make money from death. I even got money up front. I got paid to write about dead people who at the time of payment were still alive. Beat that!

I want to get off.

For an instant, I wonder if I will ever write the book. But it is only a fleeting whim. My ego was ready to overpower it. I am excited by the book. I am looking forward to having that little tablet, a paper tombstone to mark my achievement. I know it is coming, the book, I just wonder how I will bear up, having all those dead souls bound inside it. How am I going to hold up on becoming the very thing I wanted to make a stand against?

How does anybody hold up when self-reflection presents an image that he or she doesn't want to see? I guess if you are truly critical, you'll soon find yourself under Neal's putty knife. But I shan't be making any rash decisions. Death is a subject we cannot avoid and so we are doomed to fascination and wonder. Whatever edifying evidence our self-reflection throws our way, we must hope it leads to change, not death.

I need a dose of Neal. A strong dose. A dose that convinces me I have no part in any of this, that it goes on without me. I call him to arrange a good-bye breakfast the following morning. A long breakfast. A fix, one that will see me all the way home, back to my friends and family in Copenhagen.

SITTING NAKED IN THE FOREST

Today is a day of good-byes. I have said good-bye to the people in the house at Grandview Avenue. Rachel and I went out for coffee early this morning to say good-bye. She was sweet enough to buy a present for my daughter, Selma. It's a small T-shirt with a map of Twin Peaks on it.

"You can show her where you were living while you were gone," Rachel tells me as she points to the map on the T-shirt.

But I am not sure I want Selma to know. I sit here drinking coffee with somebody whose company I really enjoy, but I find it a bit awkward. I feel exhausted. I don't want to hear my own voice, which now seems so hollow and lifeless. But I try my best.

It's half past ten in the morning as I race over the Bay Bridge toward Neal's house, aware that my friendship with this bridge is rapidly coming to an end. I am excited to say good-bye. I am desperate to get home to see my family again. But, as excited as I am to be leaving, I know I will miss Neal. He has grown on me more and more with every passing day. I want to thank him for allowing me to follow his Crime Scene Cleaners and for being one of the strangest characters I have ever met. I think that for a long time to come there will be a Neal–shaped vacuum in my day-to-day life.

My phone rings.

"Alan, it's Neal. Something's come up. I can't do break-fast. Come to my house."

This really disappointments me. I really wanted to say good-bye to Neal properly. To spend a final morning with him. Oh well, I will have to make do with a coffee at Neal's house. It's not the good-bye that I was looking forward to, but there you go.

Death claims Neal's time once again.

When I pull up outside Neal's house, and turn the ignition off, Neal comes jogging out of his front door. We meet at the end of his path.

"Hey, buddy . . ."

"Hey."

"You all set to go? You taking the 5 back?" he asks.

"Yeah, I'm taking the fast route this time."

"Cool. Well, listen, anything you need, you just get me on the phone, okay?" I am expecting him to go on to say, "I'm the president of the corp," but he doesn't. Instead, with an out-stretched hand, he says, "Take care of yourself."

I shake his hand and skulk back to my car, feeling a little deflated.

But I suppose that if you like somebody for who he is,

you shouldn't be disappointed when he behaves in a way that is true to your image of him. I know that when Neal reads this he will probably say something along the lines of, "Fuuuuck! What did he want? For us to go sit naked in the forest together?" And that at least makes me smile, as I drive away from Neal's house for the last time.

I am, of course, running late on my drive to Los Angeles International Airport. Once again I am driving way too fast in a bid to beat the bushfires that keep threatening road closure when my rearview mirror is filled with the flashing of red and blue lights.

And to think, I was feeling so lonely as I barreled along.

Is this going to be my biggest Hollywood moment? Though it pains me to admit, I am thrilled by the sight in the rearview mirror. Once again I am dragged from my self-pity and find myself in a movie. In an *experience*. Because, for us Europeans, being pulled over on long dusty highways by men with guns is a Hollywood thing.

"License and registration?" the officer says sharply through the open window.

"Sure. It's a rental car, so . . ." I tell him. "I have the paperwork here," I say as I start sifting through several weeks of sandwich wrappers and coffee cups.

"Are you aware that you were doing ninety-two miles per hour?"

"I wasn't, no." Even though I know that he knows that I know that he knows that I am lying, I have started, and so I have to finish. "I thought it was more like eighty."

"Are you aware that the speed limit is seventy-five?"

Ah, that old chestnut.

"I thought it was eighty?"

"It's seventy-five," the officer says, taking an unimpressed look at the mess on the passenger seat. "Where are you going?"

"L.A. I'm flying home to Denmark."

The officer pauses. I am expecting him to ask why I am going home to Denmark when I am English. Should I not be going home to England?

This is the part of the conversation, I become aware, where I can come across as nothing else but an out-and-out liar. There is simply no way he is going to believe any of my complicated reasoning.

"Okay," he says, handing back my paperwork. "Well, slow down!"

I am amazed. He follows me for a couple of miles and then overtakes me. I watch him up ahead as he cuts across the median and doubles back the other way.

I am hoping that back home in Copenhagen, surrounded by my family and friends, I will get back to the person I was before I started focusing so much of my energy on death. But for Neal, death will continue to loom in the forefront of his mind. His views on the subject will always be guided by his work.

"Death scares the hell outta me," he had told me the other day. "But I believe there's a life after all this. I'm more of an evolutionist, but my head has a hard time dealing with the fact that we could just be worm dirt when we die."

"But ultimately it doesn't really matter if we are worm dirt," I say. "We're dead!"

"Yeah, it does!" Neal insists.

"Why does it?"

"Why doesn't it? That's the whole thing. Nobody really knows what death is. Do we have a spirit, and, if so, does that spirit live on? Do you have memory of past? Do you remember your family? Your loved ones? Do you even wanna remember that shit? I don't worry about this shit every day, but you know, when you walk in a room and Granny's a big brown spot on the hardwood floor . . . I mean, I can't accept that that's the end of it."

"Where do you think they'll be welcoming you when you die?"

"I don't think I'll go to hell. But I don't think I've *earned* heaven either. I think for the most part I live a pretty good life. I try not to bother people. I don't steal. I typically don't lie. I'm not fucking my neighbor's wife. You know?"

"But what about your views on the less fortunate? Those that commit suicide? Your views are unsympathetic. They seem very harsh."

"Dude! I didn't make them kill themselves. It's just my opinion. Suicide is for the weak-minded, my friend. It's their last 'fuck you' to everyone around them. I mean, it's my opinion. I don't preach any of it to anyone, but if you ask me I'm gonna tell ya, 'I think you're a fucking pussy. Go and blow your brains out, though. I want the money!' I don't really cram this business down anyone's throat. They come to me. If you're at the point in life where you feel you need to commit suicide, then so be it. It's your choice. I just hope they have my phone number after you do it, that's all. I am trying to run a business that makes money off that."

"If you were in a room with somebody who wanted to commit suicide, what would you say to them?"

" 'Fuck! Let me get out of the way!' "

"That would be it—you wouldn't try to talk to them?"

"I'd probably ask them, 'Why do you wanna do that?' I'd probably give them a little common sense, or try to. But you know, I'm not someone's fucking therapist. I just don't wanna be involved with it at all. But I don't have much sympathy for it. The ones I have sympathy for primarily are the old people who are sick or in pain and they kill themselves, that's fucking terrible. But I don't know if I could kill myself, man. It would have to be a pain thing, where I was in so much pain that the thought of suicide just wasn't that bad. Then how am I gonna do it? I think I'd probably use a gun, 'cause that's for sure. In most cases, like Valium, they're gonna find you, pump your stomach, and you're gonna be a retard for the rest of your life. Worm food is better than that! But in honesty, I think I'd like a slow death, even if it was painful. I would want the time to say good-bye to everybody. I don't want to be here one minute and gone the next. I want my death to be slow, like cancer. I'd take cancer—sure! Why not? Cancer would suit me just fine."

It's not something that I thought I would ever believe: that someone would *choose* cancer. But this is Neal Smither, and I find myself believing him.

For my part, I would not choose cancer, *given the choice*. Even though I have been following Neal for a while now, I have not been exposed to so much sudden death that I would take the painful, drawn-out and emotional option. I would still opt for a painless brand of death, any one will do. Now you see me, now you don't.

EPILOGUE: MAN IN THE BATH PART V

The San Quentin State Prison is spread out over 432 acres of land in Mary County, California. It was opened in July 1852 and is the oldest prison in California. The prison has 275 acres of waterfront land. It is valued at eighty million to one hundred million dollars, making it the most valuable prison in the world. California's death row is located at San Quentin. Currently, there are 622 inmates sitting on death row. Surprisingly, Jim McKinnon is not one of them.

In fact, right now, at the time of this writing, McKinnon is not even serving a sentence.

McKinnon managed to cut a deal with the DA's office after pleading guilty to voluntary manslaughter. He was released from prison in November 2007, after serving only five years in prison.

Inmates of San Quentin have included Charles Manson and the crime writer and actor Edward Bunker. One of the most notable and current inmates is Scott Peterson, who *is* currently on death row. Anticipation of the Peterson trial was already building while I was in San Francisco researching this book. I remember being in the courthouse, walking around looking for a court clerk, and hearing people in the corridors talking excitedly about the coming case.

McKinnon, I would imagine, was one of the least notable inmates in San Quentin's history. He killed a man (or do I need, legally, to call it manslaughter?), and even though he left him in a bathtub for a month, and *lived* with him rotting in that bathtub for a month, it simply wasn't newsworthy.

Or, to use another means of measurement, *punishable*.

I am at the very end now; in fact, a few years have passed since this book first appeared in the UK, when there was no end to the McKinnon trial in sight, and I find myself wondering now if I will ever really have a complete grasp on death-as-entertainment.

The fact that Gary Lee Ober decomposed in the bathtub for a month, I personally would have thought, was worth some air time. The fact that McKinnon lived in the same apartment while this was going on, I would have thought worthy of a prime-time mention.

But something about this pair, this killing, just wasn't sexy enough for the national news. The entire ordeal went for the most part unreported. Which leads me at this time to take my hat off to Ed Walsh—a journalist for the *Bay Area Reporter* who covered this case from start to finish. Walsh reported the death of Gary Lee Ober, the pretrial and plea bargain of McKinnon, and if he hadn't, where would this information be now?

Not here on this page.

The crime would simply be another act that goes un-recorded and uncared about.

Stephanie Henry cared. Walsh captured and recorded that. Henry cared, and because of Walsh, the fact that she was a friend to Ober is now a part of history. Frank Franco, the barman who pointed McKinnon out to the police, cared, too.

Walsh reported him as saying, when commenting on the parole deal, "That's just disgusting. They should leave that sucker to rot for the rest of his life."

Shortly after this comment, it is reported, Franco left the state of California, concerned for his safety.

"He's very dangerous," he told Ed Walsh. "Some other poor bastard is going to end up like [Ober]."

The reason the punishment was so light is because the prosecutors thought the case was too weak. They felt that a trial was risky. The body was, after all, badly decomposed. This minimized, or destroyed, for the most part, the physical evidence. Even though the medical examiner found two "sharp force injuries" to Ober's chest, due to the decomposition of the body it was impossible to tell if these injuries had killed him. Then there was McKinnon himself, acting crazy and setting himself up for an insanity plea.

I think most of the distress, which really seems to fan out only to Ober's two friends, Stephanie and Frank, was due to that fact that the deal was struck but not communicated. None of the key witnesses were told. The plea bargain came out only when Ed Walsh came across the information while investigating another case. He was not able to report it until two whole months had passed.

Franco was particularly upset by this. He felt it was a conscious decision on the part of the DA's office not to notify, which is normally considered standard procedure.

"It's a total slap in the face," he is reported as saying. "There's a good reason for them to keep it quiet if they settled for manslaughter. What is wrong with the prosecutors in San Francisco? It's ridiculous."

"I'm not gay. I'm not bi," McKinnon had told Ed Walsh in a jailhouse interview. "I'm a people person. And I love people. I don't like peepholes. Do you know the difference between a peephole and a people? You can see right through a peephole."

McKinnon is right. It's not possible to see through real people completely. They are always holding something back. They keep things hidden, both from those who choose to study and record them and from themselves. What real people do marvelously well, at least those who are incredibly secure within themselves, is direct all questions back to sender.

I came to San Francisco to get a look at how people live around death, to find out if Neal Smither specifically is a product of a modern culture of death or whether he is at the forefront of defining it. Even though Neal is now woven into the fabric of my story as one of life's heroes, as one of the more straightforward and painfully honest people I have ever met, it would be a push to say that he is defining some kind of American culture rather than just responding to it. He is at least ahead of most of those who feed in the wake of this culture. He is using it to his advantage, rather than the other way around.

During my time following Neal, he ended up, consciously or otherwise, working as a reflective surface. All my questions and thoughts were reverted directly back to myself. On a certain level, I think I found out more about my own character than Neal's. I found things that I don't much like about myself, and perhaps I should thank Neal for showing them to me. I am aware of these things now and can look for warning signs. But maybe I shouldn't be too hard on myself. Nobody has access, let alone an understanding, of his or her complete self. Not even Neal Smither.

I am not a classic hero like Neal. An outsider, maybe, pursuing long bouts of solitude, alcohol, and the glow from my computer screen, but that is as close as I get. Any internal battles on my part are not divided across a line of good or bad. I am not walking the same precarious path as Neal walks. I am a writer who wants to record, without influence, the lives of others. I write stories about the things other people do. My role here will always be questionable. My objective will always be hard to pull off.

We may always be looking at other people, moving toward other people, but it is only ourselves that we really get closer to. But the closer we get to understanding ourselves, the more we evolve and grow. By the time I find out who I am today, tomorrow has arrived, and I've changed again. I will never know the complete me. At least, not while I am alive.

If we are alive we always have the opportunity to change; completion comes with death and death alone. But of course, Neal throws questions even at this belief.

I remember one of my first conversations with Neal.

"Oh yeah, looky here, another scumbag bites the dust!"

he cried as we entered a suicide scene. "I'm telling you, Alan, this is pretty much what we deal with twenty-four/ seven, *scumbags*. Look at this, eighty–twenty . . . twenty-four hours, three hundred sixty-five days of the year. There's no changing them."

"What's eighty–twenty?" I asked, a little amazed at his apparent joy with how the day had started.

"Eighty–twenty's the ratio. Basically 80 percent of all the people we deal with are total fucking scumbags, the dregs of society. This is it right here, baby, and I love it. *Death*. Look at this shit!" Neal said, flicking his head toward a king-size bed where the sheets, pillow, headboard, and wall behind were all covered in blood. "This job shows you that the average person is a real shit bag. So why should I give a shit about them? I care about me and mine, meaning my family and my kid. Do I care about Johnny Dirtbag? *Damn* no! He can kill himself every night of the week as far as I'm concerned, just as long as he does it in my area so that I get paid to clean him up. Remember, this is what I do every day, Alan, I get up and I pray for death."

Remembering this conversation brings me back to Camus's theory of the absurd man. Regardless of what peace of mind accepting the illogicality of life brings us, it's not the answer. The answer, even if only in its smallest form, is to push back against acceptance. Because if you accept everything, then questions become redundant, and without questions life is finished. Take questions out of the equation and your life will be complete while you are still alive. And if death fails to bring completion, then it has no purpose, and becomes more meaningless than the most mundane of lives. You will one day come to an end with your few needed answers in place. Life will end and you will continue to drift vacillatingly forward. *You* will be absurd.

Maybe that's what ghosts are: just absurd and dead people trying to find a way out. It doesn't sound like much fun to me, to be punished to an endless existence of ludicrousness, condemned to exist between two parallel worlds. Surely, faced with such a choice, you would choose death in any of its other forms, even if that included Neal Smither. It seems to me that if you wanted proof, in one form or another, that you had been alive and had truly lived, you couldn't get anything more defining than the sound of Neal singing in the background.

Whether it's a scabby knee or a hanging head, we don't care just as long as you're dead. We'll clean on our knees happily, just as long as your check clears the bank!

ACKNOWLEDGMENTS

Thanks first of all to Neal Smither, for being a great character and for setting himself up in my mind as one of life's heroes, and to everyone on the Crime Scene Cleaners team who tolerated my lurking and occasional questioning.

Thanks also to Rachel Whiting for her friendship and hospitality and for potentially saving me from despair.

I would like to thank the following friends whose kindness, patience and guidance all went into this book: Kelly Smith, Scott Dille, Chris Lee Ramsden, Bjarte Eike, Signe Clausen, Christine Østergård (especially for the patience), and my daughter, Selma.

I was lucky enough to work with two wonderful editors on this book. Julia Rochester, from Corvo Books in the UK, who taught me a lot about my job as a writer, and Peter Joseph, of Thomas Dunne Books in the United States, who is responsible for helping me, some five years later, to take this book to a new level, one of which I am very proud.

Special thanks go to Sean Merrigan, not only for his

friendship and help regarding this text, but for the splendid drunken evenings we spent together rambling about death in all its many guises.

All transcript quotes or evidence included in the "Man in the Bath" chapters of this book refer to preliminary hearing Court No. 2068440: the People of the State of California *vs* James McKinnon.